I0015074

Social Media

How you can dominate Twitter, Facebook, Instagram and Youtube and make passive income

By Emily Goldstein

Table of Contents

Introduction

Social media networks have changed the way people connect and engage with each other. Fans and followers spend hours each day having conversations, posting messages, photos and videos, and sharing the content with one another. They share interesting and captivating information which they find useful, entertaining and valuable. That is why social media platforms are the best places to sell products, services, brands, information and knowledge among other offerings, because that is where you find your target audience.

If you want to earn money and become successful, you need to leverage social media by providing value to your target audience. Shopping has become social and so, anything you want to sell whether it is in form of products, services, knowledge or anything else, does better, if it is promoted through social media platforms. You can also earn money using other means on these platforms, whether you have a website or not. This book will show you how to earn passive income by dominating social media networks.

Chapter 1:
How You Can Dominate Social Media Networks

There are tremendous gains derived from social media marketing both tangible and intangible ones. Individuals, businesses and brands will have monetary gains, attract flow of traffic, improve customer service and public relations, as well as achieve customer loyalty and retention if they follow what is recommended in this book.

You can dominate any social media networks as long as you know what, when, where and how to do it. Promoting your products, services, or brand on social media is the right thing to do whether you are doing it as an individual or as a company. This will enable you to sell more products and services, create new customers and build an online community which you can interact with. All this can easily translate to huge profits earned passively if you mimic what other successful people have done. Some people widen their business activities to take advantage of all social media networks, but it is better to concentrate on a few networks and once you start earning from them, spread your wings to the others.

Shopping has become social

Many times, shoppers want to know other people's opinions about a product before they purchase it. They make purchasing decisions based on what their friends and followers say about the item. These shoppers seek user-generated content about the brand they are interested in buying, to find out the shopping experiences of other customers. They check the "likes", shares and comments as well as reviews and ratings on social media. If the shopping experiences are positive, they are likely to take interest in the item and if they are negative, they may lose interest. Reports show that, about 70% of shoppers, research about the brands they wish to purchase, online, to see what others have to say about them, before they buy.

To make purchasing decisions, the average shopper uses many sources of information especially from social media networks. These networks are therefore among the most powerful influencers of purchasing decisions, today. Once shoppers receive this user-generated content, they sort and filter the information based on what they consider important before they make a purchase. Retailers can leverage this by encouraging conversations to drive sales and revenue, and by participating actively on social media. This is likely to increase conversions.

Twitter

Twitter is a social media platform that enables people to read and post tweets. It was created in March 2006 and it has gained popularity all over the world with users posting millions tweets daily. The platform is used by individuals, businesses, political leaders, celebrities, company representatives, CEOs, entrepreneurs, students and many other users, worldwide. The service had over 500 million users while more than 300 million users were active by May 2015. Search queries reach billions every day and this shows that Twitter has great potential.

People who sign-up for this service are able to read and post tweets while those who have not registered can only read the tweets without posting. Sending tweets is easy and it can be done using the Twitter website, applications in smartphones and short message service (SMS), where it is available. Although tweets can be accessed by the public, users who have signed up can restrict their tweets to their followers only. These are people who have an interest in the topics they post.

Most people use Twitter as a social networking service to interact with followers, send tweets and retweets, but it is used by many other people to make real big money in ways you shall discover in this book. Twitter users share their interests with others who have the same interests. These people can talk to people who can easily relate to what they are saying. If you follow a tweeter you become a follower and you also get followers who follow you. The tweets can be retweeted over and over again, to more users until some of them become viral due to their popularity.

People who don't use Twitter at times think the users just waste their time posting details about their everyday lives. These can be tweets about what they plan to eat for dinner, their kid's special moments, their grandparent's photos, places they like visiting, how their pets behave and all kinds of things. However, people who use Twitter end up loving it and they stick with it. They use it for personal and business success.

In addition to interacting with one another and having fun, there are people who use Twitter to:

- Promote products, services, brands, businesses and organizations.

- Receive feedback in form of "likes" and comments.

- Respond to feedback.

- Earn huge amounts of money, passively.

- Find new jobs.

- Raise money for charity.

- Source for articles on various topics.

- Gather relevant information on a variety of topics among other things.

Impact of Twitter on popular brands

Social media has become a major player in retail business. Twitter and other social networks came at the right time when many companies were facing stiff competition from other major online retailers that had established themselves in the online marketplace. Social media levels the playground making it possible for any business whether big or small, to compete online. Even individuals and small-scale entrepreneurs have a chance now, to dominate social media networks and earn big money.

Celebrities are raking in huge profits as we shall see in Chapter 2 and you can mimic them to earn big bucks also. Social media turned out to be the most needed helping hand and it arrived in good time. Thanks to Twitter, Facebook, Instagram, You Tube and other platforms where retail brands can engage with audiences and drive sales. Popular brands of all types, shapes and sizes use social media to raise awareness, boost sales and revenue and maximize profits.

Twitter has a great impact on major brands like LG Electronics, Cadbury, Virgin Atlantic, Cirque Du Soleil and Porsche among many others. However, you don't have to be a big brand to gain from Twitter. Many people have reaped the enormous benefits of this platform and even small companies owned by single individuals, can take advantage of this network. Tweeting was created for people and this makes it easier for small businesses to engage with their potential customers in a personal way. Twitter is a powerful platform that is embraced by people of all walks of life. You can see people tweeting anywhere you go. They tweet to share information, follow topics that trigger their interest, and connect with leaders in particular niches, industries and politics..

Businesses can use Twitter to:

- Improve customer service and public relations.

- Generate leads and drive website traffic.

- Increase sales and revenue.

- Offer customers giveaways, discounts, daily deals and other offers.

- Communicate with their customers.

- Deepen customer loyalty.

- Get feedback and respond to it etc.

Many case studies show that, businesses can successfully use Twitter to benefit in many different ways and you can learn a lot from what others have done and succeeded. There are also lessons to be learned to avoid the mistakes some businesses experienced. Whole Foods is among the early adopters of Twitter. It has realized great success after it integrated Twitter into its marketing strategy. Whole Foods has become one of the largest retail brands that has embraced Twitter and used it to its benefit. It has successfully integrated this social network in its company goals and marketing strategy, to connect with customers and prospects. Whole Foods created more than 150 profiles in its niche, to encourage conversations and drive traffic and sales. The brand is dedicated to integrate user-generated content to drive sales. This has enabled it to have organic growth of its following and increase its blog traffic among other benefits.

Dell was also an early adopter of Twitter, and it used this platform to increase sales and meet their customers' expectations. The company realized that, Twitter was growing fast and it could benefit by tapping its potential. This had an effect on increasing and deepening its customer loyalty. It also led to better product development as a result of listening and engaging with fans and followers. Dell focused more attention on follower engagement which increased the ROI. In addition to this, there has been more emphasis on customer service, listening to customers and sales promotions, among other things they aim at with their integrated approach.

If you are looking for another great example of a business that has gained from social media ROI, then consider The Creme Brulee Man. This is a good example that proves that, social media can support a whole business. Twitter supports the value of using social media in doing business. The Crème Brulee Man is a food truck which runs in the U.S. It uses Twitter to inform customers and prospects about the truck's next location and to keep the business going. The business owner is able to reach the target audience with alerts, thus, gaining more than 12,000 followers within one year of opening the Twitter account. This is very impressive for such a small business operating on a specific geographical location. This means that, you can also use this social media platform to optimize sales and reach both existing and potential customers.

Facebook

Facebook is a popular social networking site which is free to use. It is the largest social network in the world, and it has more than 1 billion users, globally. Facebook was created by Mark Zuckerberg in 2004 and it was originally designed for college students. However, it has become so popular all over the world, among individuals, professionals, celebrities, companies and organizations. You need to sign-up right away, if you have not already done so.

Why should you use Facebook?

Facebook is a unique social media platform which enables friends, fans and the online community to share and connect with the people they care about. The interactions help you to know how your friends are doing and they also know how you are doing. These interactions have become part of our everyday life and people now expect you to have a Facebook account so they can engage with you, any time of the day. You can sign-up for free and then create your profile on the website. Once you have a Facebook account, you will be able to send messages, upload photos and videos to share with your family, friends and the online community.

You can invite as many "friends" as possible and you can become a "friend" to other people you may know and those who you are interested in, even if you don't know them. If you want to sell your products or brands on this social network, you need to send "Friend invites" to as many people as possible so that, you can enlarge your fan and follower base. Many people and businesses have embraced this social media platform making it the most popular in the world. It makes your products or services visible and gives you an online presence, all for free.

Facebook has gained so much popularity that, other website owners have integrated it on their websites to enable them to reach their existing customers and future prospects anywhere in the world. You can use your Facebook account to access many different products, tools and services which you can use, in the World Wide Web. In this book, you will learn how you can use Facebook to your advantage whether as an individual, professional, company or organization because it serves all levels. This site is available in many different languages which you can use to reach just about anyone in the world.

People who use Facebook have high return on investment (ROI) both tangible and intangible and they rake in huge profits with this free service. You can also earn passive income and enjoy the benefits

Some features include:

- Marketplace – enables you to post, read and comment on classified ads.

- Pages - allow you to create and promote your products, services or brand and the postings are available to the public. This is therefore a public page where you can post information around a specific topic. You can showcase your brand, products or services to promote your business on a Page or on multiple Pages.

- Groups - allow people who have common interests to find each other on Facebook. These people interact with each other and share information about their interests.

- Events - you can publicize an upcoming event whether it is a personal one or business-related here. It also allows you to invite guests and track down the people who plan to attend the event.

- Presence technology - enables members to view the online contacts and chat.

There are many Facebook success stories which you can learn from. Many businesses have realized tangible and intangible gains when they leverage their Facebook presence. They have joined Facebook to raise awareness of their products or services, strengthen brand loyalty, and interact with consumers directly. This has paid off in terms of an increase in sales and revenue, higher profits, loyal customers and interesting shopping experiences which they want to repeat.

Your personal profile has a Timeline/Wall where you can post and receive text, photos and videos. The Timeline is the most popular feature where friends can post their messages. In fact, it is the virtual bulletin board where you can find all kind of information. You can create a virtual Photo Album with the photos you have uploaded from your smartphone, an external camera, laptop, tablet or desktop. This is also a popular component of Facebook. Any inappropriate images or those with copyrights are usually removed by Facebook staff. Friends can like, comment and share the photos with their friends who also share with their friends. They can tag or identify the people on these photos whom they know.

Another popular feature is status updates, which enables you to broadcast announcements such as birthdays, engagements, weddings, graduations and such information, the same way you do on Twitter to reach your friends. Any interactions between you and your friends are published in the News Feed and distributed to your friends in real-time. Many successful businesses have created their Facebook Pages as their online mall from where fans can buy products, "like" them or share the information with their friends.

Popular brands whether big or small, create an online presence through Facebook Pages. You can utilize this social media platform to earn huge profits by selling your products or brands on Facebook Pages as many others have done. According to reports by IBM Coremetrics survey, Facebook has been the main source of social network traffic. More than 77% of the total social network traffic originates from Facebook. That is why it is important to setup a profile in this social media platform. Fortunately, you can sell on this site whether you have a website or not.

Clorox used their Green Works Facebook campaign to raise brand awareness. They used coupons to increase engagement which resulted in positive gains. Their discount strategy focused on page engagements with fans and Facebook advertisements. In 2011, Coca-Cola started a Facelook campaign in Israel where they placed face recognition machines to log into the Coca-Cola Facebook accounts. They could post on real life experiences at these events using just their faces only. Intel uses Facebook to discuss about technology with the online community. Intel started doing this by joining Facebook and focusing their attention on these engaging discussions on a continuous basis with their Facebook fans. They started the conversation and targeted potential fans which led to growth of their organic traffic. This widened their fan base. Although you may say that Intel is a global brand you can do what they did to increase your fans and followers which are likely to lead to higher sales and revenue.

Instagram

Instagram is an app that enables users to upload and share photos with their followers who are within the Instagram community. It also allows people to share the photos across other social media networks. The mobile app can be downloaded on iOS, Android, Windows Phone and tablets. To create your Instagram account you need to download the mobile app on your device not on your computer. After downloading and creating the account, you can use your computer to view and use Instagram. You can also sign-up using your email or Facebook account.

Instagram is a photo sharing social network that is very popular. You can use it to post your photos to your followers as well as get likes and comments. This social media platform enables you to add filters and captions to your photos before you post them. You can follow people who share interesting photos therefore becoming a follower. These may be friends, fans, celebrities, and people you know as well as those you don't know. Once you start following them, you will be able to receive their pictures, like them and share the photos with your followers.

These photos will be available on your Instagram feed where they are sent so you can view them. You should also upload and share interesting photos that you have, to attract a lot of followers to your account especially if you aim to earn money through Instagram. You can convert your followers to become your customers and start earning money for little work.

How to Participate in the Instagram Community

Participating in the Instagram community and any other social media community plays an important role in helping you to get fans and followers and in establishing your web presence.

Start by following similar accounts

The Instagram community has people like you who share the same interests. You will probably have similar accounts with them which you can follow and become a follower. You can get involved by participating and interacting with that community and ultimately you will gain followers to your account. To participate in the

Instagram community, means having interactions that are beyond uploading and sharing your photos.

To build your follower base, start by uploading your favorite photos to share with the community. They may be about you, your family, pets, memorable moments or interesting places you may have visited. There will obviously be people you share the same interests and you will also find the photos they have posted quite interesting. As you share your common interests, these people will follow you and you will follow them. However, don't follow everyone otherwise your feed may become overloaded. Choose people who post photos that interest you and start following their Instagram accounts. Once you start following them, their latest photos will be available on your feed. Follow only the accounts you have chosen that you find quite interesting.

Like the photos and make comments

You need to stay active. Once you choose the people you want to follow, take your time to "like" and comment on their photos which you find interesting. I am sure there are other people who will notice what you are doing and check your profile. This will help you gain new followers who will like and comment on your photos also. When you like other people's photos and you make nice but genuine comments, they will appreciate and feel good about it. This will prompt other people to check your profile. If you keep this trend and you stay active, it will surely lead to a steady flow of new followers to your account.

Respond to the comments on your own photos

To maintain your followers, you need to interact with them by responding to their comments. You will find some of the comments interesting, but always respond positively even when they are not. This will earn reputation. Thank the followers who have posted compliments. Answer any questions and provide details when it is appropriate. This is essential for you to help maintain your follower base.

Ask your followers questions

Use the photo caption to ask questions. This will get your comments section more active, which will attract more viewers to your photos.

Success stories of brands that used Instagram campaigns to achieve results include Capital One which used Instagram to raise awareness of its financial services and innovation to their audience. It was among the first financial services to adopt Instagram realizing a 16 point upward lift of ad recall generally and a 25 point lift from people who were more than 45 years, among other benefits. The Iconic combined both Instagram and Facebook marketing to raise awareness and drive sales of its collection. This is an online fashion retailer that realized great benefits including a 25% increase in conversion rates from social media marketing campaigns. McDonald did a summer demand campaign on Instagram and gained 47 point upward lift of ad recall. Lewis is an American retailer that sells its apparel through Instagram which made it reach over 7.4 million people.

What You Need to Do

The best way to dominate the social media networks is to join Twitter, Facebook, Instagram and You Tube among other social networks, so you can work within these platforms. This whole book shows you how you can dominate these social platforms and make passive income. However, you need to set your goals, understand your target audience, build authentic relations and engage with your followers, to lay a strong foundation and build your online presence.

Define your social media goals

It is important to set out your social media goals clearly.

- Who are you targeting or what is your target audience?

- How do you reach these people?

- How will the content you post on social media benefit them? Will it add value to their lives?

- What will you post and how often will you do it?

Setting your goals is important so you can work towards achieving them. You should choose the most important goals and work towards them and once you have achieved them, work towards the other goals.

Your social media goals may include the following:

- Gain new fans, friends and followers.

- Increase conversion rates.

- Increase sales and revenue.

- Get higher profits.

- Achieve loyalty and retention of customers.

- Get more clicks on links, tweets, video views, pageviews and subscriptions.

- Achieve more online purchases.

- Get more people to fill out contact forms.

- Signup for you newsletter.

- Downloads of your PDF file.

- Online visitors to spend more time on important website pages.

Understand your target audience

You need to understand the people you target on social media.

- What are their ages, gender, locations and lifestyles?

- Which social media platforms do they use?

- What are their buying behaviors and preferences?

- What are the channels they prefer to use?

- What are their attitudes toward similar brands, products or services?

- What value will your brands provide to them?

- What will you do differently from your competitors?

This will help you to choose the leads you intend to follow. You will also know which messages to communicate whether they will be text messages, photos or videos.

Offer value in form of content

Your main goal will be to reach your target audience by offering relevant content that is beneficial to them. People look for value. They also get excited when their friends and followers "like", share and comment on the social media posts. If you catch their attention with interesting content, this is likely to cause a buzz as they share and make comments on Twitter, Facebook, Instagram, You Tube and other social networks. They will start conversations about what you are offering them. People oftentimes like what their fans and followers also like, and this compels them to buy your products or services. But, you may not necessarily be selling anything on social media because there are many other ways you can earn money as you shall see later in this book. Make your offers available on all social networks and make your message consistent so you can send the strong signals everywhere.

Chapter 2:
Social Media Platforms

Ways You Can Make Money Using Your Twitter Account

Social media marketing has become popular and the trend shows an increasing growth. Many advertisers may target celebrities and other influencers but there is no reason why any Twitter user cannot turn to this platform to make passive income. You don't need to have a website or blog to make money on Twitter, as you will learn in this chapter. Most people join Twitter to be able to connect and engage with their followers about topics they have interests in. Twitter also offers you an opportunity to earn money.

There are several ways that you can utilize, to make money on Twitter without selling your own brands, products or services. Twitter is one of the powerful platforms where money can be earned not by just marketing other sites, but in many other ways. You can create a Twitter account in your niche or any other niche that is profitable, and then use it to make some money. It may be a niche on education, health, or family or anything you have an interest in.

Sponsored Tweets

This is a popular ad service for Twitter users that allows you earn money by tweeting ads. You will need to set your own price-per-click (PPC) for the ads that you want to tweet. You will be provided with a list of available ads which you can choose from. Choose the ads you want to tweet. The list is updated regularly. However, you should have a Twitter account, at least 50 followers and 100 tweets, to be able to sign up for this ad service.

Businesses have found Twitter to be a platform of opportunities and they use it to engage with their customers using interactions. These interactions help these businesses to create positive connections with their existing customers and followers which encourage them to send positive referrals to their followers also. The business earns money when these followers convert and become buyers or subscribers.

How Sponsored Tweets work

Sponsored Tweets is an ad platform which is used by companies to promote their brands, products or services by connecting them with tweeters. Sponsored Tweets allow companies and brands to reach prospects by having tweets sent out by Twitter users to their followers and they are paid to reach new customers. You can start tweeting ads to your followers to give companies access to your followers and you will be compensated for each advertisement which your followers accept. This means that, if you have a lot of followers and they accept the ads you tweet to them, you earn more money.

In Chapter 7 you will learn how you can increase your fans and followers who are the base advertisers use. The more followers you have especially if you are able to influence them to buy the advertising company's brands, the more money you will earn.

The only thing you need to do after you gain a wide following is write tweets based on simple guidelines which are provided by the advertiser to create Sponsored Tweets. Companies choose tweeters based on how many followers you have and the influence you have over these followers, among other factors.

If you want to earn money, you can also create attention-grabbing Promoted Tweets which are so compelling. Start by writing unique content which can be an announcement of upcoming product releases, a sale of a product or an upcoming event which you are hosting. To make the content attractive, include a picture or a video that you are sure will drive more engagement. After creating your Promoted Tweets, use the targeting options on your account settings to connect with your target audience. You can now launch your tweets engagement campaigns and the Promoted Tweets you have created will appear on the timelines of the followers you have targeted.

How popular tweeters promote brands

One of the best things about Sponsored Tweets is that tweeters have complete control. When you start creating tweets that intrigue advertisers and they vet that you have a lot of influence on your followers, they present you with great opportunities to earn money through your Sponsored Tweets account. They give you guidelines about what your tweet has to say and the links to embed in the message. In fact, when companies note that you have a wide following and you are influential, they start approaching you with attractive offers. You can take the offers you like and turn down those you don't like. This way you will be in full control of what you want to tweet and what you don't. You can be sure that money will start streaming in.

If you want to write the tweets the advertisers forward to you, use the guidelines you have been provided with by the advertisers who will approve the final text before they are posted as tweets. All Sponsored Tweets should have full disclosure, and use hashtags such as #sponsored" or "#ad. Always create messages you are comfortable with when you write the tweets. When they are approved, the tweets are posted and you receive your payment in your Sponsored Tweets account.

It is not always about the following you have on Twitter, but the influence you have on your followers. You should tweet useful, relevant, fresh, interesting, and funny content to have interactions and conversations going on. You want to contribute something useful to your followers but also something they will laugh about, Life can be stressful and it is good to pass useful information in ways that will loosen them up a bit and you can do these using free social networks.

MyLikes

This is an ad platform that is so extensive which you can use on Twitter, Instagram, YouTube, Tumbrl, your blog and other platforms. You will be able to choose ads from many advertisers, and you can schedule the time that you want the ad to be tweeted from your Twitter account or any other. You can earn $0.42 per click or much more and you get paid on a weekly-basis.

Adly

Adly is a service provider that connects celebrities such as musicians, comedians, actors, athletes, TV personalities and other influencers with companies and brands to drive sales and leads. This service helps brands to reach a wider audience and engage more deeply with the followers. Ad.ly is also digital marketing software that offers tools that boost engagement and connections which generate direct sales. Ad.ly is an ad service which allows you to send advertisements within your tweets. In this service you aren't paid-per-click like in MyLikes. What you do is that, you create your profile based on your interests, and then advertisers view your profile and they may choose your account to publicize their marketing campaigns. You then agree to send the specified number of tweets using a specific schedule, and you are paid as a lump sum.

RevTwt

RevTwt is an ad service that is Twitter-based and it helps you to earn pay-per-click. This means that the more followers you have and the more clicks they make the higher you earn. Your reputation will therefore give you more to high-paid campaigns. RevTwt is a Twitter marketing and advertising platform where you can register as a publisher to earn money.

TwittAd

Twittad is a platform that advertisers use to get their advertisements on Twitter. This is self-service type of platform which operates for coordinating the tasks between advertisers and twitter members or users. If you are a registered user you can get paid for sponsored tweets they make for the advertisers. But before the twitter user actually starts putting sponsored tweets on their account, they are matched with advertisers based on their choices.

This way the twitter users can send their desired messages to their followers. There are two types of campaign on tweet ad. In the first campaign, the user is required to tweet for the advertiser for 2 times in the period of three days, whereas in the other campaign, the user is required to post three tweets in the period of five days. Before actually sending a tweet, the user can decide his or her target audience depending on their preferences and choices. You can become part of tweet ad by signing in for free on their website.

How You Can Make Money on Facebook

Join Facebook

There are many benefits that are associated with trading on Facebook. You can setup a one-stop shop for your fans and the online community. Your customers can navigate the product Pages and make their purchases as well as go through the checkout process, without leaving Facebook. You can sell to a lot of impulse buyers especially the young consumers who have high disposable income to spend on clothing, beauty products, gadgets and digital goods especially those who are below 40 years if that is your demographic.

Facebook is one of the most popular networks used for social media marketing campaigns. Facebook focuses on creating an environment where friends, fans and followers can interact with each other and share information, photos, videos and just about anything. People form online communities within the social media network and the sharing is extended to brands, companies, organizations and the corporate world. As a result of this, you have a lot to gain by setting up an effective Facebook profile or Page. A product or service that is unique and catches the attention of the online community on social media can attract a lot of traffic whether you have a website or not.

If you want to send posts, upload photos, update your fans or place ads on your Facebook page, there are many tools to enable you to market products or services whether they are your own or you are paid to do this. These tools and the environment created by Facebook, make it possible to have a one-stop shop for the products and services you are selling.

Facebook allows individuals, companies and businesses to display information, product images, and videos to be viewed by the public. This is a very powerful social media marketing platform which you can use to make money. Facebook is the most popular social media platform and you don't want to be left behind in using it to your benefit.

Facebook offers you many choices:

- Your posts can be private or public. If they are private, only your friends will be able to view them. You can enable your privacy settings so that you keep all your interactions private.

- You can block some information which you don't want to be viewed by the public.

- Pages will be visible to the public and this means everyone who visits your Facebook Page unless you activate Privacy Settings.

- You can choose to have everyone search for your account and the information it contains, indicate which parts of your profile will be made public and what should be posted in the News Feed and determine who should view these posts. This makes usage of Facebook flexible so it is able to serve different purposes.

You can make money using Facebook but you need to create a Facebook Page(s).

What is a Facebook Page?

A Facebook Page is created for different types of businesses, brands and organizations. They use the Pages to connect and interact with their customers and share information with them. These Pages can be customized just like user profiles. They can be used to publish news stories, introduce new products and services, make announcements of upcoming events, and send other updates to existing customers and prospects. Your friends and their friends can receive your updates in their News Feed.

You can have both a personal profile and a Facebook Page (for your business). Fortunately, you can use your personal account to manage your Page. Anyone can create a Page in Facebook to sell products, services or brands and send updates to fans and the online community. This can be a source of income for you and your business. However, only business owners or their official representatives can create and manage Pages for businesses, brands, celebrities and organizations. Other people who are assigned roles to manage the Page can do so if they are authorized by the person who created the Page. This is important so that there can be control and accountability of what is posted. You can create a Facebook group if you are not authorized to create a Page. The group can create Facebook presence for the celebrities that you like or the organizations that you want to represent online.

Facebook Pages enable individuals, companies, brands, celebrities and organizations, to make regular communications which help them to interact with customers or the general public. Only your official representatives can create and manage your Page. Groups provide a space for people to communicate about shared interests. Groups can be created by anyone.

You can create and manage as many Pages as you can, there is no limit. You can tap this potential to earn money and keep it flowing.

- **Posts**: These posts on the Page and all the information on it is viewed by the public unless you have activated Privacy settings. It means that, everyone who is on Facebook can view everything you have posted. This is not bad if you are looking for fans and followers to buy what you are offering. Your posts can go viral if people like what you are selling and you can earn big bucks from a free service.

- **Audience**: Fans can "like" your Page and make comments on your products or brands. If this is shared by a lot of fans and followers, you can sell almost effortlessly. These people will receive News Feed updates on their Facebook accounts. Anyone can interact with what you have posted and so you should post interesting content and keep refreshing it.

There is no limit to the number of people who "like" a particular page and so, you can reach as many people as possible with your products, brands and services. If they like what you are selling or the information you are sending, money can start flowing in.

- **Communication**: The people you have chosen as your official representatives to help you manage your Page can create and publish posts as a way of communication with the online community. You can create customized apps such as games and contests for your Page and then use Page Insights to track the activity of your Page as well as business growth. Offer free gifts, discounts, deals and coupons to entice potential customers and win loyalty of existing customers.

You can join or create a group and use the public settings which are available to all Facebook groups. You can also create private settings for the groups. Posts of closed groups can only be viewed by group members. You may require members to be added or approved by admins by adjusting the group privacy settings. When the group reaches a pre-determined size, there are some features which become limited. If you want to set a group, the most effective groups have a tendency to be people you know.

How You Can Use Instagram to Make Money

You cannot sell your photos directly on Instagram but you can sell them through this popular platform.

Have an Instagram strategy

You always need a strategy in anything you want to do to create money for you. This is the same with Instagram and all other social media platforms you intend to utilize as a source of income. You don't just want a little money to trickle in, you want lots of it and you want it to stream in. Earning a passive income is something that many people want but they don't know how to do it. That is why you need an Instagram strategy. You will formulate a plan or strategy by answering the following questions:

- What are your goals?

- What is your niche?

- What is the target audience that you want to reach?

- What do you want to post?

- How often will you post?

Tips to help you earn money

- create good photos

- interact with the Instagram community

- strengthen your presence on Instagram

Build your follower base.

In any online business, you need traffic, if you are to start making money. This online traffic provides a market for your products. In Instagram, the products are the photos and the traffic or market, means the followers. Try as much as possible to increase your followers by uploading and posting interesting photos. Interact with your followers and discuss the photos or make comments and look out to see what others say and keep the conversations going to attract more people and build a follower base.

Utilize the hashtags

It may become difficult to reach your goals within the timeframe you have set if you don't use hashtags on Instagram. You may ultimately reach your goals but it will take a long time to do so if you fail to use them. Look for the popular hashtags or the ones that trigger interest. What will intrigue your target audience? You should use tags if you want to use Instagram content for business. A hashtag helps people to get your pictures and they widen your reach. People search for them when looking for what they need or want. You should ensure that, you use several hashrags for every photo that you post to attract more viewers. The hashtags you use should be related to the photo so they can trigger some interest. This will lead to lots of searches if the tags are broad enough.

How to use hashtags

You should have an idea of what you want to tag your picture with. To help you do this, look at the photos you want to post and note what captivates you about them. It may be the occasion i.e. birthday, wedding, graduation, the place where the photos were taken, the dress, pretty nails, hats, shoes, handbags or anything else. Tags are important because they are search terms which are used by people who want to find pictures with those specifications. If viewers search for handbags, all the pictures that are tagged #handbags will show up on search findings. This means that, you want all your tags to be relevant to your picture.

Produce quality

People like quality and if you give it to them you will be able to make money effortlessly. You can take photos with the Instagram camera on your mobile app or use your own camera. Take high quality photos and then upload them to share with your followers. You can upload them from your phone or choose them from the photo library on your tablet. You can also record videos to share with other people. Before you share the photos you can add filters, captions and your location.

You can edit a photo using effects or filters so that, your followers can have a better view of the photo. Add a caption to the photo or video and edit it if you need to. The caption can be added to the photos and videos you have shared previously or to the new ones you intend to share. Original captions you have already added to photos and videos you have shared can be edited to make them more appealing. The posts will indicate that the captions have been edited so followers can check them up.

Master the craft

It is true that most people who have an interest in your photos will only be willing to pay for them if they are good. People want value for their money and that is what you should give them. That means that, you need to master your craft by taking quality photos which are unmatched if you want to sell them for good money.

Use various cameras

You can use your phone camera or tablet to take good photos but you shouldn't limit yourself to that. You can use Instagram to upload photos that you have taken with other devices like your external camera but you have to transfer the photos to your iPhone, Android, Window Phone or Tablet first. This means that, you need to invest in a nice camera if your plan is to make huge profits using the photos which you post on Instagram. When you choose the perfect camera you will notice the difference right away and your customers and prospects will not only like them, but also buy them for good money.

Delete negative comments

The internet has some online trolls who may make negative comments on your posts. This may or may not happen but it is good to know what you can do if it happens. You can delete negative comments which people make on your posts so that your followers don't read them. You will not be able to edit them so the best thing is to delete them. You can also delete comments you have made since you can't edit them. You can delete the captions which you had added to your photos that you don't want to edit. Once you are satisfied with what you have prepared, set up your online store.

Set up your online store

Your online store is like a physical shop where people can view your pictures and buy them. You can't sell your photos on Instagram directly, so you need a storefront from where people can buy your pictures.

Services such as Twenty20 allow you to shoot photos and sell them through their site. They do the printing and shipping on your behalf for a pay. This can be a useful site if you don't want to deal with printing and shipping the orders but you can create an online store to sell your pictures directly. You can use templates to create a storefront or engage a web designer to build an e-commerce site for you.

How to Market Products for Other Companies

Gain a lot of followers

You need to have a lot of followers whom you can influence. This is important to help you to convince companies that you can impact their sales and revenue. If you want to be win contracts you will have to prove that you have the number of followers to back this up. This doesn't mean you buy these followers because companies also want to see the influence you have over your followers. Furthermore, real followers help with SERPs. You can also be penalized if your followers are not organic.

Take quality pictures

You may start marketing products or services for a company to utilize your good photography. Of course you don't want to upload average or bad photos. You have to ensure that you take the best photos of that products or services you are promoting because the work you do will influence future contracts. You should edit the photos and videos and add personal touches to make them appealing. This will make your fans and followers relate to your images instead of taking them as just advertisements.

Contact the companies you target

Get in touch with the companies you are interested in and explain to them how your Instagram account can raise awareness of their brand and attract customers. Display your best photos and videos which you have been shooting and show them the number of your followers. Let them see how often you post your updates and how you keep your Instagram feed refreshed. Make sure that you display clear, interesting and artistic pictures that can market their product and influence their customers in a positive way.

How You Can Make Money on You Tube

Create a You Tube Account and Utilize AdSense

You need to start by signing up for a You Tube account. This is not difficult if you already have a Gmail account, or if you use any products or tolls that require you to have a Google account. This account enables you to link to You Tube using the You Tube account page. After getting the You Tube account, you need to link it to an AdSense account. Google uses AdSense as the main advertising engine on all its sites and the partner sites such as You Tube. To use this service, you will have to open an AdSense account, where you will complete details including payment information, tax information etc.

Recording Your Videos

You can go ahead and create your videos. The best way to do it, is to create high quality videos with good lighting. Some people have become successful by making videos with their smartphones at home. These may be music videos or those that involve the family which are impromptu. Some of the most popular video in the market are music videos which are produced professionally. If you want to use your phone to record then using HD produces better quality content so you should ensure that you produce videos that are of the highest quality otherwise no one will watch them. To create more professional videos, you will have to use a DSLR camera together with external microphone.

Editing

After recording, you need to edit your videos. You may use You Tube free editor which has basic features. You can also use a desktop program such as iMovie or Windows Movie Maker which are free or use paid up programs such as Adobe Premiere which have advanced features. You should not use copyrighted materials like background music unless you have paid for it otherwise your videos will not qualify for You Tube advertising.

Upload Your You Tube Videos

You can now upload your videos to You Tube once you ensure that they are .....One of the ways o do this is drag and drop the videos one by one onto You Tube uploader directly from your computer. The other way is to upload them individually. This is done when you click the upload arrow. The time the videos take to upload depends on the size of each video and if you have fast internet connections. You may choose to upload multiple videos at the same time or upload one at a time. In the meantime, you may complete the information about the videos like a catchy headline, description, tags, categories, your URLs and linking the videos to your social media accounts, websites and blogs if you have them. Type as many details as possible so that the viewer can know what each video is about at a glance.

Configure Your Videos for SEO

You should know that You Tube is the 2nd largest search engine there is in the world after Google. It has also partnered with Google so any content you post on it will likely appear on search engine ranking results. You should therefore pos high quality, refreshed and relevant content that is interesting and entertaining which is good for search engine optimization (SEO). If you post content that viewers have a hunger for, they will search for it which can translate from just a few views and clicks to millions of views, clicks and subscriptions

Promote Your Videos

When you finally get your videos online, you need to let people know about them. Share the information on your social media accounts whether it is on Twitter, Facebook, Instagram, Pinterest, Google +, LinkedIn and others. Promote the videos on blogs, forums, websites, message boards and elsewhere as much as you can. Link these videos so your viewers can watch them on the You Tube channel. Avoid overdoing it so that they are not regarded as spammy otherwise you may end up having only a few or no views of your videos.

The AdSense income you get will be determined by:

- the number of views the videos receive

- the subscriptions you get

- the advertisers who show case on your video

- how many times these ads are clicked

You should aim at more engagement with the videos and the clicks you get rather than the total views although the more views you get, the more clicks you are likely to get. You can earn a lot of money on You Tube which depends on the engagements viewers have with your videos.

The best thing about You Tube videos is that, the income is passive as long as your videos are being watched. You do very little after the videos are posted. You should therefore keep track the most popular videos which perform well so that you can create other videos with similar topics. As you enlarge your video library with popular videos which viewers tag as their favorite your passive income will grow and reach levels you had not imagined.

Tip: Make videos which are entertaining, interesting or informational and you will earn good money. This is due to the fact that people are moving towards visual content rather than text. Try to record videos that viewers will watch to the end. This is because such videos will earn you more money, than those that viewers click away after watching for just a few seconds.

Chapter 3:
What celebrities don't want you to know

Major companies know that, when a celeb with a large following is associated with their products, people jump to buy them. The sales increase exponentially almost instantly as well as in the long-term, and this earns them high profits. That is why they are willing to pay the famous faces a huge amount of money because of the results they get. Ad.ly is a leading celebrity endorsement company on social media which connects the celebs with the advertisement giants. The audience is very receptive to endorsements which are presented by these stars, whether they represent organizations, companies, brands, products or services. Celebrities are among the most influential people in the world and you can follow them and other great influencers on social media, if you choose to. This chapter also contains the dos and don'ts that these celebrities religiously follow and you can copy their style.

Case Studies of Celebrities

Most of the social media traffic is driven by celebrities. That is why we need to find out what they know that we don't. Celebrities turn their fame and popularity into money whether they are musicians, actors, comedians or athletes among others. They are paid a lot of money because of who they are and the way they influence the world with what they represent. There are celebrities who have turned out to be overnight successes by indirectly vouching for different company's merchandise or their own products and services.

Money Earned From Endorsements

Various companies seek out the celebs to push their products in the market, whether they are food products, cosmetics, clothing or equipment and other products as well. They sign endorsements with these stars which make them sort of walking corporations because of earning money everywhere they go even when they are sleeping.

The highly paid celebs who earn a lot of money from endorsements include:

- George Foreman a former boxer - $ 150 million for Lean Meat Fat-Reducing Grilling Machine.

- 50 Cent a rapper - $ 100 million on Vitamin Water known as Formula 50

- Michael Jordan a basketball legend - $ 60 million per year for Nike Shoe deal royalties among other endorsements.

- Kim Kardashian – 45% of net profits of Glu Mobile among many other endorsements

- Charlize Theron an Oscar winner and actress - $ 55 million for Dior perfume

- Beyonce a pop star and entertainer - $ 50 for Pepsi among other benefits

- Justin Bieber a pop star – paid $ 12 million to design the *One Less Lonely Girl collection.*

- Justin Timberlake - $ 6 million endorsement deal with McDonald's.

These are just a few examples you can find many more all over the internet.

Money Earned From Twitter

All the tweets which are posted on Twitter are not the same. Companies pay huge amounts for tweets sent by celebrities and other famous people. They are willing to pay big bucks to these people to send a message to attract the celebrity's fan base and to promote their brands. When these big names send the messages on behalf of these companies, they also receive hefty checks. Companies enter into deals with the stars to promote their brands on social media and elsewhere. The celebs either send the tweets themselves or they have assistants and managers to do it on their behalf.

- Kim Kardashian may not reveal to the press how much she's paid to tweet but it is a hefty amount. The five figure amounts paid to her to promote products is believed to be in the range of $20,000's per tweet.

- Kloe Kardashian is paid over $13,000 per tweet and she has more than 8 million followers.

- Jared Leto is paid over $13,000 for each tweet and he has more than 1 million followers.

- Melissa Joan Hart is paid over $9,100 and has more than 320,000 followers.

- Tyrese is paid over $7,800 and has about 2 million followers.

- Snooki is paid over $7,800 and has more than 6 million followers.

- Kendra Wilkinson is paid over $7,800 and has more than 2 million followers.

- Bella Thorne is paid over $6,500 and has more than 3 million followers.

- Sean Lowe is paid over $13,000 and has more than half a million followers.

- Ashley Benson is paid over $5,200 and has more than 1.5 million followers.

- Mike Tyson is paid over $3,200 and has more than 3 million followers.

Many companies and brands partner with celebrities through social media to gain thousands or millions of pageviews and ultimately maximize their sales and revenue, which results in huge profits.

These celebrities include Kim Kardashian, Beyonce, Rihanna, Kanye West, Cristiano Ronaldo, Justin Bieber, Katty Perry and other celebs. Celebrities are paid four figure amounts for Sponsored Tweets. When celebs like Kim Kardashian sign-up for a Sponsored Tweet or a company that wants to promote their products i.e. beauty products the brand gets a huge profit because of the exposure they get. In return for being the company's tweeter or publisher, the celebrity gets a huge check.

Money Earned From You Tube

The biggest earner in You Tube has over $ 30 million subscribers.

The You Tube stars who earn big bucks on this channel include:

- Felix Avid Ulf Kjellberg using PewDewPie is a games video commentator who earns $7 million per year from You Tube videos. He has over 33 million subscribers and more than 7 billion views.

- YOG SCAST Lewis and Simon on You Tube earn $6.7 million per year from You Tube videos. He has over 7 million subscribers and more than 2.9 billion views.

- Antony Padilla and Ian Hecox on Smosh comedy earn $5.7 million per year from You Tube videos. He has over 19 million subscribers and more than 3.9 billion views.

- Disney Collection Toys Collector makes the owner earn $5 million per year from You Tube videos. He has over 3 million subscribers and more than 4.5 billion views.

- BluCollection Toys Collector makes the owner earn $4.8 million per year from You Tube videos. He has over 1.5 million subscribers and more than 2.6 billion views.

- Jenna Marbles is a popular You Tube personality and Comedian earns $4.3 million per year from You Tube videos. He has over 14 million subscribers and more than 1.6 billion views.

- TobyGames earns $4.2 million per year from You Tube videos. He has over 6.9 million subscribers and more than 1.8 billion views.

- Comedian Ray William Jr. earns $4 million per year from You Tube videos. He has over 10 million subscribers and more than 2 billion views.

These people have become viral raking in millions of dollars.

When companies sign endorsements with celebs they do so for the following reasons:

- To extend their reach to a wider audience

- To reach fans and followers

- To maximize their sales and revenue

- To optimize profits

You can also earn hefty profits if you copy or mimic the tactics these celebs use. You will know the dos and don'ts that make celebrities stand out on social media and you can mimic them to become successful.

Celebrities are paid thousands of dollars for a single photo snap shared on Instagram to promote products, services, brands, companies and organization. The exploding popularity of Instagram has become a source of money for celebrities and non-celebrities. The Insta-celebrities are earning big bucks through this service. Many users are connecting with big companies by selling sponsored photos to them. You can tap this potential because the growth of this industry is overwhelming.

How Celebs Use Social Media to Promote Themselves

Social media has become a major part of our everyday lives and celebrities are using it for self-promotion. For the last few years, celebrities have earned huge profits and we should copy their tactics to earn money. They use Twitter, Facebook, Instagram and You Tube among other social networks to interact with their fans and gain a lot of followers who look out for their updates. Social networks can be used as an effective marketing tool either for self-promotion, charity or to promote products, services, brands and companies.

Most celebrities leverage social media to promote themselves and charity. Because of their popularity, they gain a lot of fans and followers who follow them to get updates. Their fans and followers seek their profiles to get updates about their lives, upcoming events, the latest news and what they are up to. Their thoughts are posted on tweets while their latest photos and videos are posted on Facebook, Instagram, and You Tube. This means that, celebs have the best opportunities to market themselves to a wide audience. When promotions are done well, this can result in a lot of fun for celebrities and their fans who may not even realize that it was an advertising campaign.

The public interact on social media sending large crowds to Facebook Pages, You Tube clicks, followers' tweets and much more. When these interactions go viral and the results are tremendous. As an individual marketer or advertiser, you can tap this opportunity to make huge profits by interacting with the crowd as you showcase your offerings. Celebs like Kathy Perry use their performances to gain not only followers but huge sums of money from their shows. They gain followers they didn't have before and receive feedback about their shows from fans and this strengthens fan loyalty.

Rihanna is another favorite on social media who uses her Facebook page to engage her fans during her album releases. This gives her a lot of publicity, millions of followers, and album sales that earn big bucks for her.

Some celebs earn huge profits from wearing designer clothes, shoes, hats, handbags and other items. A celeb can be paid as much as $250,000 to wear a designer dress and appear with it on the red carpet.

Tactics Celebrities Use Which You Can Copy

You may want to earn money like the celebrities but fail to. You can mimic the celebrity success although you may not reach that point but you can earn yourself enough money that comes easily. I am sure you wouldn't complain if you earned some few dollars here and there for doing little work. Anyone can use these techniques.

Become popular

Celebs are popular personalities but you don't have to be a celebrity to gain popularity because even a viral tweet or an interesting photo or video can start you off in the journey of fame.

Get a lot of fans and followers

What drives business online is traffic. If you manage to get a lot of fans and followers, you will smile all the way to the bank. Social media is usually thought to be for personal gain, but it can be used to earn money by businesses whether large or small. Celebrities reach out to their fans for support using social media and to notify them of upcoming events and new projects. They share new information to get their followers talking. Gaining millions of followers needs consistency and patience. You don't just win them over in a few days unless you cause a buzz of activity to speed up the process. As you gain new followers you should spread the news about your products or services.

Give exclusive value

To mimic celebrity success, you need to give exclusive value to your fans and followers on social media. People like value and if you provide it to them, they will have a reason to pay attention and to pay money for what you offer them. It is important to sell quality products and services which your customers will value. Back this up with exclusive content on social media in form of interesting and entertaining text messages, as well as high quality photos and videos. People look out for brands that will solve their problems or enhance their lives. If you offer these to them especially what other people don't offer, they will come looking for you instead of you looking for them.

Utilize the influence that you have

We can't all be powerful influencers like celebrities, but we all have a chance to prove ourselves. Use social media to do this, and start with the influence you already have. Invite as many friends and followers as you can because there is no reason why you can't have loyal followings regardless of your business size. Rally your followers behind you and what you are offering and unite them for a certain cause.

Involve and reward your biggest supporters

Reward your supporters personally. This is something that the most successful celebs do regularly. They also send "Thank you" messages as they interact with their fans. They reward their biggest supporters with something special which they also appreciate. This may be a free musical download, a coupon code, or mentioning them on Facebook, Twitter or other networks. This sends a buzz as people try to find who those people are and what they did. You can copy this technique by recognizing your most loyal supporters and rewarding them. Include them also in your social media campaigns so that they can feel special. Everyone likes a pat on the back or a word of praise when they do something good. They will become thrilled and use word of mouth to spread the news and this could gain you new followers and money as well.

Don't become offensive

One of the don'ts that you learn from some celebrities (not all) is that, don't become offensive or annoying. Words make and they also break. People have different cultural backgrounds, beliefs, languages, religious affiliations and attitudes. Anyone sending an ad should be careful about the words used so he or she doesn't become offensive to the target audience and the general public. That is why market analysis should be conducted beforehand.

Don't overdo things

Some celebrities overdo things and they go beyond themselves. If you want to attract attention from the right people, then stay sober and cool. You will gain more by so doing than otherwise.

Think beyond yourself

Many people say that success is not success until you have helped someone else. Celebrities reach out to help other people. They use social networks to promote a cause and to raise donations for charity. This makes them popular and they gain more followers who support them in what they do. Extend your hand to someone in need or support causes like preserving the environment. There are many things you can do but always think beyond yourself in whichever way you can. Make an impact however little that is, and make the world a better place to live in.

Many social media sites can be used not just to have fun but to make huge profits. Your followers can be a source of money. Advertisers may want to reach to your fans to sell them their products or services. People who have a huge following on sites like Twitter keep in touch with their fans. They also get paid by advertisers for sending ads to their followers. Celebrities make a lot of money on social media. They are paid huge sums of money.

One way they earn money easily is by tweeting and retweeting. Some even earn per word on the 140 character tweets. They don't even have to write 140 characters to earn their money. A company that wants to get online visibility can ask a celebrity to tweet about the product. Millions of people believe in the message sent just because it was sent by a celebrity and they buy the product. The company makes a huge profit and the celebrity earns a lot of money.

Celebrities are paid to tweet but the difference between them and other tweeters is that they are paid huge sums of money. Some make thousands of dollars per tweet which translates to a lot of money per word on the 140 character tweet. They may earn through Sponsored Tweets or use a service like Ad.ly or any other service. They may even tweet directly, but the profits they make out of it are tremendous. They make a lot of money by doing less work.

One of the ways some celebrities and non-celebrities follow which you can also do is to put the ad in a compelling language. They use the power of words. This may be an ad about a shampoo they used, a weight-loss program or anything else, but the words they use are so compelling that, they appeal to the target audience and the public with their enticing words. You can use enticing words which people want to hear but you have to be genuine. There is no point of promoting a product that you know for sure will not deliver. You need to promote quality and value. The product may take long to penetrate the market but once it does, it will stay competitive.

Celebrities sell their photos and videos on social media for huge profits. For many stars, they earn big bucks on these platforms by promoting products or services which people rush to buy. This is a great way to make money. They sell photos and movies that are used by marketers and advertisers to publicize their upcoming projects and events. They make thousands of dollars for a photo used to promote a product.

Celebrities previously used Instagram to post their fabulous looks but today they use it to earn big real money. Kim Kardashan, Beyonce and all the celebrities we have mentioned have thousands of followers, who producers and advertisers tap to make money by selling their brands through these celebrities. People believe that once these starts endorse the brands they are over high value and quality.

Endorsements of products and services

Celebrities and famous people earn a lot of money through endorsements of brands, products and services. They may make the endorsements directly or they may use services such as Mobile Media Lab that connects popular photo snappers with the large companies in different industries that are willing to pay for these endorsements.

If you have over 100,000 followers on Instagram, you can earn $700 to $900 for a single photo. If you have let's say 500,000 followers, you can earn $2,000 to $3,000 for one picture snap that is used by companies and advertisers to thrust their brand on your followers' eyes. There are even celebrities or fashionable Instagram users who earn $8,000 per sponsored snap. For celebrities who command millions of followers on Instagram, you cannot even guess how much they earn. They sign huge contracts that pay huge profits for their insta-endorsements.

There is money to be earned you only need to get as many followers as possible. Companies pay you higher rates if you have more followers on social media than those who don't.

Chapter 4:
Branding- shape up or ship out

Branding is used in marketing and advertising by successful businesses all over the world. Branding is so important that, you have to shape up or ship out. It means that you either do it or you are out. In this chapter you will know what branding entails, the psychology of color, and why some brands are easier to remember than others. You will know why some brands are so popular while others are not. You will know how to create catchy profiles, videos, tweets and other content that online visitors will find interesting and entertaining.

Fans and followers that convert, search for certain content in the social networks and if you give it to them your success is almost obvious. You will see things you need to consider when you are branding your products, services, business, company or organization. This will become clear in this chapter, to help you offer your fans and followers what they are looking for.

What Branding Means

The American Marketing Association (AMA) defines a brand as a "name, term, sign, symbol or design, or a combination of them intended to identify the goods and services of one seller or group of sellers and to differentiate them from those of other sellers".

The different Brand elements

A brand, whether it is in form of color, name, logo, shape or any other type, communicates its message and meaning to the target market. Color evokes certain meanings even when it is used without words. Our minds are programmed in a way that we react instantaneously to color. That is why we stop at the traffic lights when they are red and move on when they are green.

Brands typically comprise various elements, such as:

- Name: this is the word or words you use to identify your product, service, company, or business concept. You should choose a unique, short and simple word or words as we shall see later that is easy to spell, type, pronounce and remember.

- Colors: are very effective as a brand such as the blue used by Facebook, Twitter, LinkedIn, IBM and Dell among other leading giants.

- Logo: this is the visual trademark which is used to identify different brands. Get a graphic designer to design your logo which people will relate with your brand. Choose the colors you want to make your brand stand out from the rest. A logo can be used with or without the name (s) of your brand or company.

- Tastes: you can associate the unique taste of fried chicken sold by Kentucky Fried Chicken which is the company's brand. The unique recipe for fried chicken is comprised of herbs and spices which has been trademarked by the company. When you taste the chicken, you know right away it is Kentucky Fried Chicken.

- Graphics: are used for branding, such as the red ribbon used by Coca-Cola. When people see the graphics even from a distance, they know what they represent. If you want to use graphics, choose something unique.

- Shapes: can be used such as the shapes of Coca-Cola bottles and VW beetle which are only used by these brands. You can trademark shapes that you want to be used to identify your brand such as circles, triangles, oval, rectangles, star-shapes or any other.

- <u>Sounds</u>: can represent a brand like NBC unique tune. When people hear that tune they associate it with that NBC.

- Other brands include taglines or catchphrases, movements, numbers, the letters in the alphabet, symbols and different kinds of pictures.

Color and psychology

Brands use the psychology of color to convey brand messages with or without words. Some brands are easily recognizable by their single color while others use a combination of colors. Brands that use favorite colors especially blue are popular among social media users. Color is the single visual component that most people easily remember. This is followed by shapes, symbols, numbers and finally words. If the word is simple, short and easy to spell as we shall see later in this chapter, it becomes easier to remember.

Logos also represent specific brands just like many trade names. A logo is a visual representation of the brand with or without a name. A single image conveys a lot of information almost instantly. People perceive the image at once and so they are able to process the information within a short time. The bird on Twitter and the "f" on Facebook which represent these social media giants are popular and easy to remember. The AT&T logo is also popular and it represents electronic communications around the world.

A good brand:

- Conveys the message clearly

- Connects the target audience emotionally

- Motivates buyers

- Confirms the business credibility

- Ensures user loyalty

Color and Branding

Branding will make it easier for the target audience to find your content. It is therefore important to choose the right color(s) that represents the message you wish to convey to your target audience.

Color is powerful and it influences our everyday lives. It can change your moods, feelings and behavior in many ways. Color can make us to relax, be playful, feel warm, buy more or less, take action, eat more and do much more. It has great impact on people's lives. This depends on what they associate with a particular color. The color you use can trigger certain actions or reactions because it has a personality. You can use color to trigger emotional connection between your customers and your brand.

Color creates reactions in everyone of us. It can make or break your customer experiences. The colors you use on your brand evoke customers' reactions and this determines whether they will buy your products or services, or not. If you want to attract the right kind of clients and customers, you have to use the right colors. Color is your silent sales force. You can gain an advantage for your business using color.

Branding vs. Marketing

Oftentimes, branding is taken by many people to mean marketing. Although marketing may contribute to branding, the two terms aren't the same. A brand should be bigger than any marketing efforts or campaigns. The brand is what you remain with after the marketing campaigns have been concluded. This is what sticks to people's minds relating the name, color, logo etc. with a product, service, company or organization whether these people bought the product or service, or they didn't. Some people buy what you offer right away while some buy later, but what is important, is for them to remember your brand and to ensure that it appeals to them emotionally. This way, they will buy and keep coming back for more.

Brand determines whether someone will become a loyal customer or not. Although marketing may convince people to purchase a particular item, they may buy it only once if there is no branding. If there is branding and the brand sticks to their minds they will keep purchasing the product or service time and again. At times, they may buy only that brand for the rest of their lives. These customers may also check other products or services offered by the same company because of the trust, reliability, safety and dependability they associate with that brand. That is why branding is so important. If you want to succeed in branding, you need to understand the needs and wants of your target audience. This includes your existing customers and prospects.

You should define your company's brand strategies and integrate them at every point where your brand gets in contact with the public. This way, your brand will stick to the hearts and minds of your customers, and prospects.

Social Media Branding

Most of the popular brands in the world are recognized instantly by color. Research shows that, people are mostly able to say whether they are attracted to a message or not based on the color alone. Color therefore makes a brand easily recognizable even whether other elements are not used. However, there are some colors that are endearing to online users and blue is such a color. When you are branding, it is important that use the right color for your needs.

Blue is the world's favorite color

Why do you think the major social networking sites all use blue color or shades of blue as their branding color? Do you think this is a coincidence or it is clever branding? It is not a mistake that all social media giants chose blue as their primary color in branding.

Research has shown that, blue is the world's most popular color and it is therefore not a wonder that, the sky and the sea are blue. We are surrounded by blue everywhere we go. Both male and female chose blue as their favorite color according to research studies and so, it is unanimous that, it is the world's favorite color.

Blue is the most popular color in social media branding and it is not a coincidence that, Facebook, Twitter and LinkedIn all use blue or shades of it, as the primary color. Brands use blue color to appear calm and logical. Blue is cool like the ocean.

What color Blue means

Blue color is used by companies that represent trust, integrity, and communication. No wonder it is used by major social media sites which build trust and are often used for communication. Blue also represents calmness like the ocean and the sky. It makes you feel calm just by looking at it. Blue is related to the mind and that is why consumers often relate it with communication and logic. However, the right tone of blue is necessary because if the wrong shade is used, it can make the brand to appear cold and unapproachable.

The brands that use Blue

The major social media brands such as Twitter, Facebook, and LinkedIn use blue as the primary color in their branding. Other companies that use blue are Microsoft, IBM and Dell among others. There is a lot of Blue in Google also. The light blue tone used by Twitter and the bird logo express the fun side of social media while the blue tone used by Facebook shows that it is trustworthy, dependable and reliable. You can use blue color in social branding if you aim to communicate with your online customers and the social media community. However, this doesn't mean you can't use other colors.

Blue Color Psychology

Blue is referred to as the color of the mind/intellect which makes it the color of communication. This is why it is used by social media sites because they are all about communicating. Blue also represents brands that want to be perceived as safe, reliable, trustworthy and dependable which are positive qualities of any type of business that chooses to use blue in the branding. Blue is also used in most laundry detergents and bleaches to symbolize cleanliness and the calmness you feel in clean clothes and a clean environment. Most football teams use uniform colors as a kind of branding to symbolize the companies they support.

When choosing the blue shade or tone, you should carry out an analysis to find the right one for your needs. Whatever you choose should correctly reflect your brand values in all ways.

Choose the Right Colors For Your Brand

You have already seen what blue represents. However, there are many other colors you can choose apart from blue. The color you choose to use should represent the message you want to convey to the audience you target and the general public. What will these people see when they come in contact with your brand? You may choose a single color or multiple colors to represent your brand. Each color is interpreted differently and so you should know what people expect in order to know you have chosen the right color.

Red

Brands use red to represent how powerful and passionate they are. You can use this color if that is the message you want your target audience to receive.

- <u>What Red represents</u>: Red is referred to as the color of power and passion. It also represents excitement, energy, and courage.

- **Which brands use Red**: Red is used by Coca-Cola and the Virgin Group among other brands. They are some of the biggest and most powerful brands in the world which use red to symbolize energy, excitement, confidence and power. Red is the Valentine's Day color that conveys passion.

Green

Brands use green to represent Mother Nature and to show their youthfulness. If that is what you represent, then green is good for you.

- **What Green represents**: Green represents the environment, Mother Nature and universal love. Although it is also the color of money it mainly symbolizes the environment. That is why "Go Green" is a popular phrase among those that want to preserve the environment. The youth are also attracted to green and all those people who enjoy life.

- **Which brands use Green**: The green on Starbucks shows its responsibility to preserve the environment. The coffee company is earth-friendly and this is represented by its brand, all over the world. Many products that are made of natural produce or flavors use green to represent Mother Nature. If your target audience is the youth or your brand has some youthfulness values, you may choose green.

Yellow

Brands use yellow to symbolize fun and friendliness. If that is what your products or services want to portray, then yellow may be the right color for you.

- <u>What Yellow represents</u>: Brands that use yellow express happiness, friendliness and optimism. Yellow is so visible during the day that it is hard to overlook it. The brands that use it are easily recognizable even from a far. Marketers use this color when promoting brands that show excitement.

- <u>Which brands use Yellow</u>: McDonald's uses yellow in the big "M that stands out against the blue sky high above. The contrast of yellow against the blue or white (clouds) is hard to miss. It pops out above the streets as you drive by. Other brands that use yellow are Google and

IKEA. In some instances like IKEA the color shows that shopping here is a lot of fun and people will have a happy experience.

Black

Brands use black to signify exclusivity and glamour. Black is also a neutral color which can be used to add value to other colors. It can also be used as a background color in order to highlight other colors used.

- <u>What Black represents</u>: Like purple, black can also be seen to represent luxury and glamour. When this color is used correctly, you can use to represent exclusivity and sophistication. When black is used whether in brands or elsewhere, the color is taken seriously.

- <u>Which brands use Black</u>: Brands that use black include the gold and black logo of Gilt Groupe. Others include Chanel and Yves Saint Laurent sporting brands.

Orange

Brands use orange to represent warmth like fire, some kind of playfulness like in children's playgrounds and also physical comfort.

- <u>What Orange represents</u>: Orange is a powerful bright color which company brands use to indicate fun, playfulness and an enjoyment of social interactions. Orange can be used to stand for physical comfort and warmth. However, you should be cautious when using orange, because your brand can be taken to mean that you don't take things seriously. Orange also represents speed and energy like in FedEx to denote the kind of transportation to expect. Orange is also used in laundry detergents to indicate their dynamic energy and power.

- <u>Which brands use Orange</u>: This color is used on TV network Nickelodeon Kid's program where the brightness of orange represents kid's having fun. This is important because kids get excited when they see the program. The ING financial institution uses orange in their brand but contrast it with blue to reduce the playfulness representation

Pink

Brands that use pink want to deliver the message that, they are sweet although it depends on the pink used.

- **What Pink represents**: Pink is a feminine color although it is also used by men especially during weddings i.e. tie. The color represents certain qualities such as love, caring and nurturing. The light pink is used for little girls who are usually sweet and adorable. It is therefore used to market products meant for babies and small girls. Women use pink to show their feminine nature.

- **Which brands use Pink**: Victoria is a pink-branded company which even promotes PINK products among their line of products. Many charities such as Susan G. Komen, which are related to breast cancer use pink to raise awareness and encourage prevention of breast cancer. This organization and many others support those who have this disease and those who have overcome it. They also wear the pink awareness ribbons and ask others to do so, usually in October to promote Breast Cancer Awareness. Pink Cancer Awareness Ribbons are recognized all over the world,

Brown

Brown is the color of the earth and it is used by companies and organizations to represent warmth and dependability.

- <u>What Brown represents</u>: When brown is mentioned as a brand, what come to mind is chocolate whether it is a chocolate bar, chocolate cake, drink or cocoa powder. The meaning of this color is warmth, reliability, safety, and dependability. You may use it if that is what your brand stands for.

- <u>Which brands use Brown</u>: Brown is grounded within the earth and it is used by UPS in different tones. It symbolizes the trust the company promises as it delivers customers' mail and packages on time. It is easy to identify the M&Ms sweet chocolate brand that comes in brown packaging and gives the consumer those warm feelings associated with chocolate.

Purple

Brands that are luxurious use purple.

- **What Purple represents**: In branding, purple stands for luxury, quality and royalty. However, this color can sometimes be interpreted as tacky, whimsical, or out of touch with reality, depending on the user. This can become detrimental to the message that you want your brand to send.

- **Which brands use Purple**: A brand like Cadbury's uses purple in its trademark which goes well with the rich chocolate that is contained in its products.

Tips

When one color stands out in the background, it becomes unique and this makes it easy to recognize. Men prefer shades of colors whereby black is added while women prefer tones whereby white is added.

Important Things to Consider When Branding

There are several factors to consider: Color as we have seen is a determinant of whether your brand will be effective. The following are other things to consider.

Your target audience

Define your target audience. Is it adults or children, male or female, youth or the aged? What you are targeting whether it is business or consumer sectors. Is your business a business to customer B2C or business to business B2B type?

Product or Service

What do you plan to sell to your target market? Is the product or service going to meet a need or it is a luxury item or service? Is it something your customers are willing to save money to buy immediately or they will purchase at a specific time? Does it have special features that make it appealing? Is it for impulse buying or customers are saving to buy it?

Customers

What do they like or dislike about your current product or service which you need to change?

Strategy

How will you attract your prospective customers to your products or services?

Age

The age of your target audience or demographic: Are you planning to sell to children, teenagers or adults? You don't want to sell products or services that are meant for adults to children because it won't be suitable for them.

Gender of your target audience

Is it male or female or both? You wouldn't want to sell female products to the male because the response might be poor.

Location of target audience

Is it urban or rural, cities, towns or country, international or global?

Income level

The income level of your existing and potential customers is important. You need to determine what your customers can afford especially if you are dealing with luxury items.

Brand image

What do your existing customers think about your current brand? This is how your customers think about the brand in their mind when they see or hear about it. The image is created in the minds of people when they come in contact with the brand. This is the sum of all the information and expectations which people associate with your product, service or company.

Brand identity

How would you want them to think about the brand? You need to bridge the gap between the customer's brand image and your company's brand identity.

Competition

Who are your competitors that are likely to win your prospects' loyalty and devotion?

Types of brand names

Brand names have many styles which include:

- Initials: a name like IBM and UPS can consist of initials.

- Description: a name like Wonder Foods can describe the product or its benefits.

- Founder's names: you can use the names of the founder, such as Dell, Disney or Hewlett-Packard.

- Combination: you can combine multiple words to create one word like Microsoft which is microcomputer and software, Comcast which is a short form of communications and broadcast or Vodafone which combines voice, data and telephone.

- Foreign word: the word can be used from another language, like Volvo or Samsung.

- Alliteration and rhyme: are fun names which are easy to remember such as Dunkin' Donuts.

- Evoke an image: Names that evoke an image, such as Amazon.

- Geographical location: these brands are named after geographical locations and landmarks.

- Made-up words.

- Personal: brands take personal names i.e. Betty Crocker.

- Punny names: some brands use puns i.e. Lord of the Fries, Wok on Water etc.

How to Make Your Brand Memorable

As you do your branding always remember that it is PR that builds a brand and make it known. You need brand awareness and brand communication to spread word far and wide.

Short name

Short names are easy to remember. The shorter a brand name is, the easier it is to remember and type. When the name is long and complicated it becomes difficult to remember. When you easily remember the name, then it becomes easier for you to search it online because many people can type it without making errors.

Short brand names include Nike, Coke, Gap, Apple, Rolex, Crest, Tide among others.

Long names include Abercrombie & Fitch, Morgan Stanley, Deloitte & Touche, Bausch & Lomb etc.

Simple

A simple name is easier to pronounce and spell. Short isn't the same as simple. A name can be short and yet quite difficult   Simplicity has to do with the alphabetical construction of a brand name. A simple word uses only a few letters of the alphabet and arranges them in a combination that repeats itself. That is why people easily remember Mississippi (4 alphabets) unlike a name like Schwab (6 alphabets).

Simple brand names include Google, Coca-Cola, Nissan, Facebook, You Tube, Pinterest, and Twitter.

Easy to Spell

An easy to spell name is memorable although not always. Avoid using a combination of letters and numbers or adding symbols because it can make it difficult to spell or remember. If people can't spell your brand name correctly when searching online, they may not get your website or blog.

Easy to spell names include Facebook, Amazon and Old Navy.

Difficult to spell names include Daewoo, Abercrombie & Fitch, Hyundai etc.

Category

A name that suggests the category of your products or services, can help customers identity your brand easily. You can shorten the generic name or create a proper name that is easy to remember i.e. Nilla for Vanilla ice-cream. You can also use a word that suggests the category i.e. PlayStation etc.

Unique

A unique name can be very effective and easy to remember. Unique names can also be short, simple, easy to spell and easy to pronounce..

Unique brand names include Xerox, Sony, Kodak, Kleenex etc.

Alliterative

The sound of a brand name is more important than the way it looks since our minds work with the sounds of words. Rhyme something to help customers remember it.

Alliterative names include Jelly Belly, Dunkin' Donuts, Volvo, BlackBerry etc.

Easy to pronounce

To make your brand effective, you have to consider the importance of word of mouth. Make the name easy to pronounce and friends, family, co-workers and neighbors will be talking about it. It will be in everyone's lips. This is more powerful than any advertisements you may do.

Easy to pronounce brand names include Subway, Target, Polo and iPod.

Difficult brand names include Isaac Mizrahi, Chipolte, Dasani, Hoechst and HSBC.

Personalized names

You can personalize your brand name to make it easy to remember.

Some great personalized brand names: Dell, Papa John's Pizza, and Disney.

Effects of Branding

A brand can be very effective. When branding is done properly it can lead to higher sales and revenue. This can happen to your product, and other products associated with your brand. Although brand development can take time, effort and resources, it is worth it. Clients and customers will not only buy the product you are promoting but oftentimes they will also buy others products from your company because they trust your brand. This is the effect branding has on your business.

The brand is the personality that makes your customers, fans, friends and followers to identify your product, service or company. It is the name, term, sign, symbol, design, or a combination of any of them that relates the product service r company with the customers, employees, partners, investors and other stakeholders in your niche market. These are people who are linked to your brand in their thoughts, feelings, attitudes, perceptions, beliefs and experiences.

When your customers come in contact with your brand when they are viewing it, buying it or on advertisements, this is known as brand experience. The team that is engaged in branding try as much as possible to align people's expectations with their brand experience, so that they create the impression that the product or service represented by the brand is unique or it has special qualities. Branding is therefore can therefore valuable in marketing and advertising.

When you carry out careful brand management you make your products or services relevant to your target audience. You ensure that, what you promise is what you offer to the people you are targeting. Your brand represents the valuable qualities you offer to the consumer.

Your brand can gain so much recognition that people in the target market can state which one it is without being exposed to the company's name. These people base their recognition of the brand with logos, color, trademark and slogans, is s a measure of success and the effectiveness branding has on your product or service. A brand that is widely known and can easily be recognized is said to have brand recognition.

Chapter 5:
Calculate and Track Your ROI

In this chapter, you learn about how you can track and measure your return on investment (ROI) and the tools and metrics you can use. You will be introduced to various tools like Google analyzer and how you can use them to identify whether your user base likes your products and how to catch their attention if they don't like them.

You will know how to use demographics, interests, behaviors, mobile and technological factors to see where their converting traffic come from, why they visit the websites, and what they are interested in. This will help to know where to spend more money on and which areas to give more attention. You will also know how you can use conversion reports to help maximize conversions of site visitors among many other things.

ROI is generally expressed as a rate of return meaning how long it takes to earn back what you invested. When you say that the annual ROI of is 20% (percent), all it means is that it will take five years to recover what you put invested. This a straightforward formula where money is involved but when it comes to social media campaigns, it takes more than money to become successful and for your time and efforts to pay off. If you are employed you may hear your boss complaining that you spend too much time on social media. When you are working for yourself, you know that you have to spend a lot of time posting tweets, messages, photos and videos to catch the attention of fans, followers and the public. If you don't do this, how else would you earn ROI? I am sure you would want to pay yourself for all that time and efforts in addition to the money you have invested.

ROI may be ignored by people who don't like dealing with business finance but a look through this chapter will make them think otherwise. Tracking and calculating your ROI can become exciting and at the same time challenging. The greatest challenge may be the way algorithms keep changing from time to time. These are the algorithms which determine the factors to be used to track and calculate ROI. There is a way to deal with this variable, in order to get the best results which you can depend on.

Return on Investment (ROI)

Your social media ROI will contribute towards your profits making a positive effect to your bottom line. Many marketers and brands may still not know how social media drives return on investment (ROI) but if they read this book, they will see how they can do it to their benefit. You can leverage social media to earn huge profits if you know how to do it. As you shall discover in this book, your social media investment is warranted paying you back with profits. You may spend money, time and efforts on social media, but when this increases your profits, you will be glad that you took this social path. You need to track how social influences the interaction you have with your customers.

Businesses use social media return on investment (ROI) to measure how their social media investments pay back and how much they get from social media marketing efforts. This is investment in terms of resources, time and efforts. ROI is measured in form of money or as a percentage of what you invested. It may intrigue you how the social media likes, shares, tweets and retweets can be calculated in dollars and you will see how as you read on. Social media platforms such as Twitter and Facebook are free to join and you can utilize these social marketing channels among several others to make passive income. It should be exciting to know that, you can make huge profits out of these social networks like others have done. To know if you are making money, you need to track and measure ROI and you will learn how to do this in this chapter.

How to Measure Social Media ROI

You may spend a lot of your time and efforts on social media marketing campaigns without knowing whether you are successful or not. Your clients who have given you business or those that intend to, may constantly require proof of your return on investment (ROI) and the best way to win them over is to give this to them. To prove that your investment on social media is warranted or it is worth it, you need to track and measure ROI. This will show you how social influences your interactions with your clients and the online community. After all you also need to measure your success and know what you need to improve on. You can either increase your return (income) or lower the cost of investment or do both to impact ROI positively. If you don't measure your success, you won't know how well you are doing and this is like walking blindly. You therefore need to find a workable strategy that enables you to measure your social media ROI regularly.

To build your business, find customers and make money on social media, you need to make data-based decisions and find out what the ROI on the social actions you take. This will enable you to decide which social actions are the best for your business. This helps you to know which valuable social media actions you need to emphasize. You will know where to invest more time and money, and what to focus on. Some marketers and advertisers may have missed this all along wasting a lot of money with little to show for their hard work which makes them feel frustrated. This is due to the fact that they spend a lot of time trying to track and measure factors that keep changing all the time. They also find ROI elusive because of the different activities that take place on different social media platforms. You need to concentrate in the right areas and use Google reports.

To track and measure ROI you need to:

- Identify the investments you have made on social media in terms of time, effort and resources which need to be monetized. The main resource used is oftentimes money.

- Know how much you get from each social goal you have chosen, in monetary value.

How to Calculate ROI of Your Social Media Marketing Efforts

ROI is a business metric which is used to measure the effectiveness of social media marketing campaigns.

ROI=Return minus Investment divided by Investment

There are 2 things to this equation

- Return is what you have gained from investment.

- Investment means cost of investment or the expenses you have incurred.

The cost of investment means more than cash. It includes the time and effort you or your employees have used on social media to earn the return. All the factors need to be converted to money form. Example: the hours you have used tweeting, posting messages on Facebook, shooting and posting Instagram photos and You Tube videos should be calculated. How much would someone else have been paid for hours you have spent and the efforts you have put? Estimate the hours and use the current rates you would have used to pay another person to do the same work. This is your own time and efforts as well as that of the assistants and managers who post on social media on your behalf. Some major company brands, celebrities and famous people employ assistants and managers to post on their social media profiles and manage their business Pages and accounts.

You can either calculate social media ROI for a specific marketing campaign or for a particular product or you can measure it for a whole year based on the income and marketing expenses.

It is also good to have comparisons between ROI of several forms of marketing which you have adopted so you can know what needs to be emphasized. This can be a comparison between the net revenue returned from social media investment and SEO returns or paid-up advertising like Pay-per-Click. This may sound hard to some people but there are tools to help you do that. Track and measure ROI every month, quarter, and yearly, although this depends on the parameters you are measuring. This will keep you well-informed and have everything at your fingertips. You will know when and where to put more resources, time and efforts. Once you start earning from social media, you will be motivated to make the calculations regularly to beat competition and stay ahead of your competitors. This will be an adventure and you will enjoy the journey once you know how to influence the results.

Tips to measure social media ROI

In order to know if your social media efforts are paying off you need to follow the tips we have provided and use the tools we have recommended.

Why should you Measure Your ROI?

Measuring ROI is proof that your marketing efforts are effective. Companies and other clients need to know whether you are successful or not before they consider...... and you do too. This is important for social media companies, consultants and in-house staff. The main challenge in measuring ROI is keeping up with changes in algorithms, implementing the new tools that hit the marketplace and proving to your clients that they're getting the most out of their investment in you.

How to calculate your return on investment

Many people calculate social media ROI based on performance metrics such as increases in:

- The amount of traffic to your website or to your social media pages.

- The number of online conversations that includes a positive mention of your company.

- References to your company versus references to your competitors

- The number of people who join your social networks or bookmark your sites

- The number of people who post to your blog, comment on your Facebook timeline, or retweet your comments

These measurements may be worth monitoring, but they're only intermediate steps in the ROI process.

Investment in the form of money i.e. dollars

Performance metrics include:

- The action taken i.e. tweets

- The reactions i.e. retweets

- The non-financial impact

How you can calculate your Return (income)

Return may be trickier to measure than investment but you can still do it. This is due to the fact that different marketers may have their own factors that determine the return on social media ROI. The term return can mean different things to different people depending on what they want to measure. Furthermore, their ROI goals may change from time to time and as a result, change the variables. For the calculation to become easier, you need to know what you want to achieve with social media. What are your social media goals and which goal is more important than all the others? Is it gaining new followers, having online sales or more clicks on links? You need to specify the right actions that meet these goals? Calculate how much these actions are worth to you in terms of money and this will be your Return.

1. Specify your goals

There is a wide range of goals which you can choose from. You can choose a combination of goals from the following possibilities and many others. Once you specify a goal (or goals) it becomes easier for you to know what you want to track and measure. Social goals may include conversion goals or the desired actions which you want to be performed by your visitors.

- Gaining new followers

- Clicks on the links

- Increased online purchases

- Higher sales and revenues

- Signup for your newsletter, news feed and other subscriptions

- Filling out contact forms

- More time customer spend on product webpages

2. Track your goals

You need to track and measure the goals you have chosen with Google Analytics i.e. sales, time spent on pages, downloads, signups. You can also track social media interactions i.e. likes, shares, and your followers using a social media management tool like Buffer, Hootsuite or Everypost.

3. Monetize your goals

After choosing the goals and having tracked them, you need to convert them into dollars or other currency.

There are several different methods to choose from here:

- **Lifetime value** means the amount you earn from a customer or prospect(on average).

- **Conversion Rate** is the rate you would use if you hired someone else to do the work.

- **Lifetime value** can be multiplied by the **conversion rate** to get how much potential clicks, visits, pageviews etc. are worth to you.

- **Average sale** is the average online purchases made on your website or the sales you gain from your social media efforts.

- **Price-per-Click, PPC costs** is the amount which you would have paid if you used ads to achieve the same social media actions. This is the same amount you would pay for advertisement to gain a click, a new follower, a PDF download etc., and then you use this as the amount you would pay yourself for organic social media likes, shares, posts, and impressions which you do.

You can get the amount it costs to gain a prospect by checking how much on average a Sponsored Tweet costs, a Facebook like, a You Tube click etc. You need to know how much it costs to win a new fan or follower. If it is $20 and you win 100 fans or followers then your organic gain is $1,000.

How you can calculate your investment

While it is true that social media participation is free and you can post on Twitter, Facebook, Instagram and on other social sites for free it is good to remember that the time you spend is not. The social media tools you use may also not be free. If you pay for similar advertisements, you may spend quite an amount in actual dollars. You time and efforts are investments just like the money you have spent on social media campaigns.

Your time: You should multiply the average labor-cost per hour, with the number of hours you have worked on social media for a specified time. This will depend on whether you want to measure social media ROI for a week, month, per year or per campaign. You may check how much social media managers are paid at an hourly rate. You can use Glassdoor to check salary levels of social media managers.

Social media tools: You can do this by adding up all the costs of the tools and services you use for your social media campaigns. If you want to measure monthly costs all you need to do is to divide the annual costs by 12 months. For weekly costs, you will divide the annual costs by 52 to get the weekly costs.

Advertisement costs: This is the amount that you spend paying for advertisements on social media that promote tweets and boost Facebook posts, instagram photos and You Tube videos among many other ads.

When you add all these costs together you will get the cost of investment.

Since you now have the return and investment, you can now use the following formula:

ROI=Return minus Investment divided by Investment

Tools to Track and Measure ROI

Success on social media is achieved through a strategic plan that includes testing what works best for you and what doesn't. This helps you to make the necessary adjustments to achieve your social media goals and the overall business objectives. If you are to succeed on social media channels, you will have to understand how people interact on these social networks and find ways to engage your target audience. You should sign-up for Google Analytics to help you track customer interactions and the effect this has on your social media ROI. This will help to strategize how you can engage your target audience even more.

Google Analytics

You should sign up for Google Analytics to start your site's traffic. Google Analytics is a web analytics service which helps users to track and report web traffic visiting their sites. It is offered by Google among other products and tools. This is a very effective web analytics service and the most widely used on the internet. You should adopt it and use it to know whether people like your products or services and know what you should do if they don't. By using the information provided, you will be able to make informed decisions and take corrective measures if people don't seem to like your products or services. This should be timely. You may offer quality products or services that add value to people's lives, but, it may be the way you present them that doesn't appeal to your fans and followers. You need to improve on this or any other constraint you may have.

When you sign-up, you will get a tracking code to paste on your website pages so Google can know when your site get visitors. If you have an e-commerce website, Google will use the tracking code to track transactions and calculate revenue and ROI.

Google Analytics has been integrated with AdWords in a way that, users are able to review their online campaigns by tracking conversion and other elements like the quality of landing page. Your goals may include increase in sales, sign-ups, pageviews, lead generation, time duration viewing a specific page, or downloading a particular file

The approach that Google Analytics takes is to provide straightforward data that is helpful to a casual user and more detailed data with in-depth information and analysis, for advanced users. The pages that perform poorly are identified so users can know what they need to do about them.

Google Analytics Social Reports

You may spend time each day having fun and pass time on social media and most people do that, but when it comes to making money as a business, you need some serious time.

Funnel Visualization

This enables you to identify your traffic sources.

It shows you:

- from where your online visitors come from i.e. social media referrals

- how long the visitors stayed on your site

- their geographical locations

- segmentation of your custom visitors

Google Analytics has an e-commerce capability that sends reports about the sales activities and performance that it has tracked.

This e-commerce reports show you:

- All your site transactions

- Sales and revenue generated

- Other related metrics

Real Time Analytics

This was launched by Google Analytics to help users get information on real-time.

Cohort Analysis

This is a Google Analytics feature which you can use to help you to understand other users that are not within your usual user population. You will understand their behavior so that you can be able to design and implement your market strategy with these user groups in mind. Many analysts and marketers find this a beneficial tool.

Google Analytics Content Experiments

This tool is integrated in Google Analytics. It was previously known as Google Website Optimizer which was a free website optimization tool that tested different types of content. Webmasters and online marketers used this tool to increase conversion rates and visitor satisfaction. They could also test the entire page or test each factor separately. They could test the impact of headlines, products images, product copy, calls to action, product reviews, fonts, and other variables.

Google AdWords

AdWords has evolved to be a major revenue earner for Google.

Conversions Report

Conversion reports help you to understand how visitors to your website or blog convert and what you can do to influence these conversions to your benefit. The conversions report helps you to know how you can optimize your site or social interactions for higher conversion rates. You can use this report to create a desirable ROI. The main metric that is used to measure ROI is money. If you get that insight, you are on the right track.

You should have conversion goals which you want to track. You will also be able to follow the path which your visitors take from the time they enter your website all the way through to the time they make purchases or become leads.

Some of the information you will get includes:

- Goal completions are the total number of all the conversions you have realized.

- Goal value is the total value of achieving the goals you set up. It is calculated as the total goal completions multiplied by the value you assigned to each goal.

- Goal Conversion Rate is the average rate used after summing up all conversion rates.

- Total Abandonment Rate is the rate at which visitors abandoned goals.

The Social Conversions Report enables you to track and measure the success of the social campaigns you have undertaken and to improve your marketing efforts. This allows you to allocate the returns to each social media network and align the success to each social goal. By looking at what each network returns in terms of ROI you will know which social media platforms add the highest to your bottom-line. You will understand what you need to concentrate on to bring you profits and what you need to overhaul. If Twitter is the one giving you more profit, them put more time and money in it, if it is Facebook, then spend more time and efforts there. You will also know what on-site social goals make in terms of returns. You will know which social goals and ecommerce transactions work for you and which ones you need to go low on at least for the time being.

The Conversions Report helps you to justify why you need to spend more time and money on social media networks and which ones.

The reports show:

- the number of conversions which are attributed to your social campaigns

- the value of these conversions in dollar amount

- the social networks which bring in conversion value

- which social networks bring more conversion value i.e. Twitter $ 300, Facebook $ 250, Instagram $ 200, LinkedIn $ 50, HootSuite $ 20 etc.

The reports can be further broken down for each network into i.e. assisted and last interaction conversions both as rates and in dollar value.

You can now see which networks bring the highest ROI and which campaigns are most effective. You will therefore know which networks you need to put more time and money in, and which campaigns work best for each social media platform.

The Goals Overview Report

The Goals Overview Report shows you at a glance the total number of the goal completions on your site. This is usually where you are making money. You can view where your converting visitors come from and see which pages goal completions take place.

Goal URL reports show the URLs where your site visitors convert. If you use Destination Goal you will see on which page the visitor was before going the Destination URL. This may be a confirmation page or Thank You page where visitors land after goal completion.

Reverse goal path reports show you the most popular paths which are used by your site visitors to complete a goal and how many steps they take to complete a goal. You may want to shorten the path so your visitors complete the goals much faster.

Social Value

<u>Assisted Conversions</u>: This conversions take place when people visit your site and leave without converting. These people don't convert immediately, but they convert later when they make subsequent visits.

Last Interaction Conversions: This happens when people visit your site and converts right away. These visits are considered last click conversions.

This will show you whether social has helped to trigger the conversation or it has led to the real value as site visitors close the deal. You will also identify the networks which are better for assisted social conversions and which ones are best for last interaction social conversions which translate to generation of overall traffic.

The Social Sources Report

The Social Sources Report is used to identify the social networks and online communities which visitors use while engaging with your content. It also lets you to see how different people interact with your content depending on where they come from. This report shows you where you should devote your resources, time and efforts. By looking at your analytics, you will see which network generates more traffic for you and how long visitors stay on the site. Most of your traffic may come from Twitter while visitors on Facebook may stay longer on your site.

This may have formed a trend where visitors from Facebook may engage with your content for longer periods of time. These people may dig deeper into your other site pages. You can use these analytics, to know those visitors that easily convert and at what rates. You should concentrate your resources on networks that visitors use to engage traffic and generate more conversions.

Other important tools include Hootsuite, Salesforce, uberVU through Hootsuite and Custom URL.

- Google Analytics You can use this tool to track your website's traffic, conversion rates, and sign-ups that happen as a result of social media campaigns.

- Hootsuite: This is a tool that offers a variety of analytics tools. These tools will help you to track your social reach, conversion rates and other metrics.

- Salesforce: This tracks sales that arise as a result of social media messages or posts and specific social marketing campaigns when you add tracking codes to the links that you share on social media networks.

- uberVU through Hootsuite: This will help you to know the share you command in your industry related to social media, your reach and other measures concerning your brand.

Chapter 6:
SEO- Deliberately Make Yourself Noticed

Search Engine Optimization (SEO) is very much a vital technique when it comes to social media largely because of the mammoth searches conducted every minute. These searches make SEO on social channels a crucial part of running any type of business. You can therefore imagine the impact social networks have on your bottom line. You should deliberately make yourself noticed because it is only by so doing, will you enjoy the great advantages that go with social media. It is like a physical store, by displaying your goods where people can easily see them your prospective customers will pop in and buy them. If your store is somewhere where it is not noticeable, you will need to put extra effort to advertise it. This is the same thing that happens online. You need to be visible and one of the ways to do this is to work towards SEO.

In this chapter you will discover how you can deliberately make yourself noticed by using key SEO techniques that you can start employing right away. The essential SEO concepts that many successful companies use in marketing products and services will be explained. There will also be tips that will help you to raise awareness on social media as well as maximize sales and revenue.

You should work on SEO because your existing customers can easily reach you but prospective customers may not even know that you exist. You need SEO to make your business visible and increase its search engine rankings. Popular search engines like Google analyze, index and rate websites regularly. If your website or offerings appear on top of search engine rankings they will be discovered by potential customers. However, you may not need a website because you can sell your products or services on social media. Either way, you need to work on SEO, to make you and your offerings noticed.

Tips You Can Follow to Gain from Social Media SEO

The internet and the use of mobile applications whether in form of smartphones, tablets, iPhones and iPods have eased communication, globally. This has made people to engage and connect on social media networks than ever before. If you want to succeed in your online business today, you need to reach your target audience where they spend most of their time and that is on social media.

SEO is a very effective online marketing tool which increases your visibility and you should therefore adopt it. Social media has become the most effective and cost-saving channel to make you noticed.

Increase your engagements with fans and followers

You should engage and connect with your socially connected customers and as you do Google will notice you. Search engines put a lot of importance in these social media networking engagements and so you should post more content and ask your followers to like, share, reply, tag as favorite and comment on your posts because this will help search engine indexing and raise your search rankings higher.

This is an era of social media and you should align your business objectives with the needs of your fans, followers and the online community because they influence each other in decision-making. You can do this by utilizing social media networking sites. You can promote your website using social media but you don't have to have a website. You can post your content on Twitter, a Facebook Page, Instagram photos, You Tube videos, Tumbrl and Pinterest whether you are selling a brand, products or your services like tweeting to earn money.

A business which is socially optimized gets on top of search ranking where it becomes noticed by the target audience and as a result, it attracts a larger flow of traffic than the one that is not. There are more interactions on the social networks between friends, fans and the online community. These people market the business across the social media networking sites like Twitter, Facebook and other sites and this can lead to sales and generation of revenue.

Increase social signals

Google has been using social signals more than any other factors to index and rank websites and other places where content is found. That is why it is important to increase your online friends, fans and followers and their engagements with you and your content. The input of the online community has surpassed all those other marketing messages that were used in the past.

Social signals influence SEO because search engines look at these social signals to find out:

- how often you post content on your social media accounts

- how many people interact with you and your content

- if you have social-sharing elements available to visitors to your site.

There's no point in trying to outsmart the algorithms with fake likes on Facebook.

Add social buttons

You should add social buttons on your website so site visitors can recommend the site to their friends and followers on social media. The social media "likes", "shares", comments, links, favorites and other engagements are used by Google in their ranking results and they help you to gain points and climb higher on the ranking results.

It is common to find Facebook, Twitter and Pinterest buttons on most websites. You should exploit these opportunities to be able to generate generic links which are rewarded by the search engines.

Use Links and Inter-Links

Add your website links and URL address on all your social media profiles You Tube, and Facebook pages. On the other hand, interlink all your social media accounts i.e. show your other social media accounts i.e. Twitter, Instagram, You Tube, Pinterest on Facebook and so on.

Encourage social activity

You should encourage fans, followers and site visitors to engage and interact with each other on your social media accounts and send feedback. Respond to the feedback to increase activity. Encourage your fans and followers to leave comments on their social media profiles or join in the conversations. You can do this by choosing words, photos and videos that will excite them to evoke their emotions. If they become emotionally attached to your content, they will be comfortable enough to share their experiences with others. Google indexes such social activities and so you should encourage more conversations.

Post quality content

The quality of content you post on social media, on your site and if you have a blog determine your SEO success whether it is in form of images, videos, tweets, or other types. Make it high-quality. You should motivate your audience to interact with you by using enticing or inspirational words. Add interactive content that triggers conversations and sharing. It should be informative, interesting and useful to make people want to share it.

Increase lead generation

Lead generation on social channels is not the same as what other methods use to push the sales messages. You cannot oversell or push people to buy your brands on social networks because it is rarely appropriate. If you want to be successful in your lead generation, you need to think like a social person rather than a marketer. Think about what you would want as a social customer and not as a salesperson or marketer. You also need to help your prospects to solve their problems and answer questions that intrigue them. Show your customers that you care about them and what they care about. Make sure that you get involved in the conversations and keep monitoring what goes on. If there are questions, answer them and respond to criticisms in a fair manner.

Tracking

Social optimization is vital in any online social activity especially when it involves the public. You should test and adopt social media strategies that will attract more traffic by tracking and measuring these activities.

Companies use SEO to catch the attention of the target audience who look for keywords and web content to search what they want. If your content is SEO oriented it will attract traffic to your website that are likely to convert to loyal customers. When a potential customer enters a keyword, your website appears among the top rated sites, so the customer can see it and click to see what you are offering.

Shortcuts to boost SEO with social media

SEO makes your products visible in the online marketplace. If you have to get your products noticed by online shoppers and get an edge in the competitive online market, you need to adopt. In this chapter you will discover ways to boost search engine optimization using social media. You will learn how you can improve your SEO and the key techniques you can use.

Make your content interactive and engaging

In order to catch the attention of search engines and online visitors, your content on social media has to be interactive and engaging. This will attract search engine rankings and place your offerings in a position that prospects will notice you. This will help you to keep site visitors interested in what you offer get an enjoyable experience which will make them come back to buy from you over and over again. As a result, your sales and revenue increase and your profits soar.

Grow your follower base

Any profiles and Pages that have a lot of high-quality followers usually rank higher in search engine results. Google and other search engines look for real followers on social media channels who they regard as high-quality followers especially those that interact or engage with you. You can be sure that if the online community likes what you offer, a large percentage will engage or interact with you in one way or another. To increase your Google authority use likes, shares, retweets, replies, favorites and comments.

Use relevant keywords in your posts

Although Google can penalize you if you use keywords excessively, they are still important for SEO because this makes it easier for search engines to match your keywords with your content. When people use words or phrases to search for what they want in the online marketplace, it appears on their search findings. You should therefore find out what your target audience is searching for in your niche so you can include these keywords in your social media posts and on your website, blog and any paid advertisement campaigns. If you do, you are likely to rank higher in search engines results.

Do keyword research using Google Adwords to bring traffic to your Pages, channel, website and blog if you've listed them in your profile. This ensures that your content is searchable. When users search for these keywords, your content shows up and they can then click it.

Optimize your content and updates on social media

In order to optimize your content on social media, you should post updates. When you refresh your content, Google indexes the new content much faster and this can lead to a higher ranking position. You should also share content that you have on your website or blog on all your social media posts to boost SEO. Use keywords or phrases that describe your business and the terms people are likely to use when searching for your brand, products or services. Include the name of your business in your social network posts so that Google can relate the keywords with your business.

Twitter and Google struck a deal and became partners. It is most likely that, the content you post on Twitter will be indexed by Google which is good for you. Since Google has the highest traffic globally, you will be able to attract traffic to your website and Twitter accounts easily. There is also a higher chance that, users who see the content on Google search, will click it.

Encourage external inbound links

Link building is an important SEO technique. Social media encourages external inbound links from external sites. These links should be high-quality. High-quality, authoritative content means higher SERP ranking. You can create links on social media or with your website to website relationships. Inbound links are valued by Google and they appear for indexing. Try to have more quality inbound links by having valued sites linking to your website and also link to other quality websites to get outbound links. These links are more authoritative on Google and you can be rewarded with high SERP rankings.

Post authoritative content

Google ranks authoritative content highly. This includes social media likes, shares, comments, retweets, photos, videos, and repins among other content. You should create content that people want to share, comment on and like. This can be posts which people find interesting, useful and trigger their emotions to want to share the content with others. The content has to be interesting so that engage with you, with the content and with other people. Search engines value these engagements. You can add social sharing buttons to all pieces of content to increase engagements.

Make all your content searchable and sharable

Social media networks encourage sharing of content. You may choose privacy settings on Twitter, Facebook, Instagram, You Tube and Pinterest for your personal account but when it comes to earning money you need to choose the option that enables search engines to search your content, on your social media profiles.

On your Facebook profile you have the option of making your Facebook posts searchable by search engines and you can do this by activating your settings. When more people see the posts on your Page, the more people will want to share it. Encourage sharing of content by asking for likes, comments and shares to trigger interest because this will increase your search engine rankings. Ask fans and followers to share the content with their friends and followers. Post contests on your Page or start a Page specifically for the contests. For business, you need to make information available to the public and this means all your social accounts should be public. Ensure that all your content is searchable and sharable.

Use social channels to build high-quality links

Social sites such as Twitter, Facebook, Instagram and You Tube command a high authority right away. Your Facebook Page may rank higher than your website even if it is just a new one. This is due to the high authority Facebook and these other social media platforms commands. That is why you need to ensure that, your links appear on all your social media profiles.

Sign up for Google+ and spend time every day on it

To make your brand social, it is important to sign-up for Google+ Business Page. Ensure that you complete the "About" section and other fields with as much information as possible especially with keywords which describe your business. Google allows you to add links (which you have customized) on your profile which is good for your business. You can use this opportunity to link to your website, You Tube, blog, and other social channels. When you spend a few minutes each day sharing your content on your Google+, you will likely appear within Google top search rankings.

Create Local Listings on Google+

You should have a local listing on Google+ and include your address in it. If you do this, prospects will be able to review your business directly on Google. Another advantage is that, Google recommends businesses which have the highest reviews. On top of this, have a list of your location or a map for your business on your Facebook page. Not only can it be helpful for social media, but it also makes it easier for customers to find you and check in. This is great for local SEO. Social media can make a big impact on your search rankings. To make your online store successful and boost organic search engine traffic to your site, sales and revenue you need to work hard on search engine optimization SEO.

Utilize Google My Business

Google My Business connects you to customer. This enables your business to become visible to customers. Your business information is put on Search, Map and Google+ so that prospects using all types of devices can easily find you.

Use Mobile Marketing

Mobile marketing has become an important part of business today as more people use smartphones and tablets. This trend is expected to in the future. You should make your posts, blogs and websites available to mobile shoppers on different types of devices. Ensure that the sites are easy to navigate, the checkout process s easier and the load times are minimized to encourage mobile shopping.

Build your following

The number of followers you have gives you authority on Google and other search engines. Take into consideration the authority your domain has by checking the following that you have on social media platforms. Build this following by posting interesting material regularly, and engaging your audience directly. You can do this by responding to their comments and questions, and by opening up public discussions around a topic that is sought by fans and followers. Post updates multiple times in a day.

Build organic following naturally because Google can detect when your following is real and when spam.

Make use of Google AdWords

You should optimize your keywords by utilizing Google AdWords keyword tool which is free. This way, you will be able to get keyword phrases that are suitable for your products. Each product type has specific keyword phrases that the online traffic is searching for. When you type the search phrase of your choice, Google AdWords keyword tool will show how many searches are generated by that phrase. It will also show other alternate phrases and the traffic they generate. This way you will be able to pick the best keyword phrase for your products that is effective.

Emphasize local posts and keywords

Social media provides you with a perfect opportunity to contact and engage with your local community. You can send specific posts and keywords that target your local community to the major search engines. There are times when competing with major brands in search engine rankings may not be the right thing to do especially if you operate your business locally. You may want to concentrate on a specific geographical location, to capture the online traffic searching for local keywords. In such instances, local posts and keywords should be emphasized that are relevant to the local community. This improves your ranking position making your business more visible because online visitors search for posts and local keywords which they easily relate to.

Send posts on social media, when your company gets involved in local events such as tradeshows, local festivals and other events. Take photos and make posts, which invite local residents to like, share and make comments. Interact with other popular brands on social media and learn from them.

Optimize your domain name

Choose the perfect keyword rich-domain name as a search engine optimization SEO strategy, is key to success. Use short and simple domains that people will remember easily. As you saw in branding, complicated words make it hard for existing and potential customers to remember. It also becomes difficult for them to type on search, so they may never find your website or content. Include keywords relevant to your brand in your domain so people can easily find you, your products, services, website or blog. Display your keyword-rich URL, on all your social profiles and accounts. A short and simple keyword phrase is easy to type and remember. If you want your website to generate traffic, start with the right keyword-based domain name and make it search engine-friendly to gain from SERPs.

Avoid using too many keywords

In the past, using too many keywords helped your site or content to appear higher on search engine results, but this does not happen anymore. Using many keywords will make your content appear like it is spam and this can be penalized by Google and other search engines. Avoid stuffing your site with too many keywords in the content, title tags, alt text, product descriptions and links. Use similar words or phrases to attract search indexing.

Avoid duplicate content

Duplicated content is a common problem which can adversely affect your search rankings. Avoid overlapping pages, titles, tags, multiple categories and keywords that results in duplicate content. You should avoid all duplicate content because you can be penalized by search engines.

SEO is important in getting you top rankings, attracting traffic to your site and increasing conversions. You should therefore strive to improve SEO.

Chapter 7:
Ways to exponentially increase your fans and followers

The total number of fans and followers that you have and the way you engage with them, has an important part to play in determining your success on social media. This has a significant role in search engine optimization because it influences your search engine rankings. Google can now be able to detect the quality of your followers and whether they are real or not. This means that, sourcing for followers by purchasing them as businesses used to do may because you more harm than good.

Low-quality followers lower your search engine rankings. You should therefore make sure that, you have real people as your followers, who interact with you and with the content you post. Google notes these interactions and indexes them. You need to build organic following otherwise Google might penalize you with lower rankings. Increasing the number of your fans and followers may be a slow process, but you will learn effective methods that will make it easier for you in this chapter.

Tactics You Can Use to Gain Fans and Followers

- **Advertise**: Start by advertising your brand, products, services or company on your Facebook fan page, Twitter account, through Instagram photos and You Tube videos as we have seen in the previous chapter. You may display your offerings in form of text messages, photos and videos. Ask people to like them, share them, and post comments. Ask You Tube viewers to subscribe to your videos and tag them as favorites. As more people do this, they notice you and become your followers.

- **Rewards**: Reward your fans and followers who "like" your posts, those who follow you and those who fulfill your desirable call to action. Offer those people who support you free gifts, discounts, coupons and other offers, to encourage them to keep doing what they do in order to promote you. Sending them "Thank you" messages and mentioning them, will keep them coming back. Celebrities and company brands that are influential do more than just post content. They actively engage with their fans and followers almost on a daily basis. They send thank you messages to those who support their campaigns. They may do so personally or engage managers and assistants to do the follow-up.

- **Catchy headlines**: Having catchy headlines with unique and interesting titles is important. Your photos, videos, product descriptions and other content should have catch headlines and titles. Tag the keywords on the descriptions so they can be searchable. This will make people who find them follow you if you offer value and if you solve their problems.

- **Unique content**: High quality photos, videos and posts are particularly popular. Keep refreshing them and add your own comments and captions to trigger interest of followers.

- **Fan engagement**: Engaging with fans will make their friends and followers to find out about your offerings and they may follow you.

- **Contests and projects**: You may consider posting contests and projects on Facebook Pages (and in your other social accounts) whether they are your business

Pages or you have created specific Contest Pages. However, you cannot post Facebook contests on your personal timeline.

- **Post hot issues**: People have a hunger for hot issues in the news. If they know that they will get this information on your social media accounts, they will always seek for the hot news and follow you. You can search news and link them to your social media accounts so people can click them. They will be browsing your accounts to get more. This way, you will gain more fans and followers.

- **Respond to feedback**: All feedback is important whether it is positive or negative. It makes you know how you are performing. Respond to feedback in a positive way even when they are criticisms. This way, you will intrigue more and make them follow you. However, you can delete negative comments which won't add value.

- **Updates**: Keep updating your products, social media pages, videos, photos and posts. Once you have posted your content, keep refreshing it. Post new product photos and videos and add new comments. Edit comments and add more captions on your photos and videos. Fresh content attracts search engine indexing.

Strategies You Can Follow to Gain Fans and Followers on Twitter

Are you ready to attract more followers on your Twitter account? Make Twitter your top priority for some time and create a lot of content. You don't need to be a celebrity to gain followers on Twitter or to establish yourself in this community. All you need is to follow the proven strategies that successful people have followed which are set out below. These will help to increase your visibility and make you worth following.

The following are effective strategies which have been tested and proven to be effective.

Target popular tweeters: There are people who have massive following in your niche or industry. Find them and follow them so their massive followers can notice you and follow you. Popular tweeters attract a lot of attention. If you follow these people, you will catch the attention of their followers with your likes, shares, comments, jokes and the conversations you have and your fans and followers will increase.

Follow famous people: You may choose to follow tweeters who are generally popular, and you will see them on the Twitter website. You can see the number of their followers, following and tweets. Celebrities, TV personalities and famous people like Katy Perry, Justin Bieber, President Barack Obama, Taylor Swift, Rihanna, Justin Timberlake, Ellen DeGeneres, Britney Spears, Christiano Ronaldo, Kim Kardashian, Jennifer Lopez, Oprah Winfrey and many other popular tweeters have millions of followers. If you want to follow them, you can click the follow button on Twitter website. You will also get a list of global icons on the Twitter website, that have high following, and this will help you to see the best tweeters in your field, industry or geographical location.

Work on your profile: Put an avatar of a photo showing your face or head shot and write a good bio. You can use your brand as your avatar instead of using your photo. Your account may appear to be spammy if you use images and graphics that you pick at random. Avoid this because it is not recommended. People will read your Twitter bio before they decide whether they want to follow you or not. Create a good bio that is properly written and complete all the details. People will want to know who you are and what your interests are before they follow you.

Follow those who follow you: On Twitter it is expected that those people you don't follow might unfollow you. That is why it is important to follow all those people who follow you. You have to do this carefully otherwise it might be counter-intuitive when you focus on gaining a lot of followers because you might lose some of your followers. The advantage is that, some of these people might respond and make their followers follow you so you have to weigh between what you might gain against what you might lose.

Create interesting tweets: The tweets should be interesting, funny, useful, informational and at times provocative but not in a bad way. These tweets will make people start talking and as they talk about the topics, some will choose to follow you to read more tweets. So, the better the tweets, the more followers you will get.

Be interesting and transparent: Share news about yourself and your life experiences. You can spin an interesting story, so readers can get glued to your daily life and the unexpected dramas that take place every day. Most of your potential followers will look at the tweets you have posted, to see if you are worth following.

Solve people's problem: Find out what problems people are having and post useful content that will help solve their problems. Offer solutions and useful information. This adds value to people's lives and you will find them following you.

Add variety: Avoid posting boring content. Tweet about different topics instead of sharing only about your everyday life and your personal thoughts. This may be about your interests, hobbies, insights or spice up the content with a photo about something different.

Be active: Tweet as often as you can at least one or two posts each day and do it consistently. There is no one who wants to follow someone who doesn't tweet. When you become active and consistent, it becomes easy for you to maximize your visibility.

Tweet at the right time: Choose the right time to post your tweets. This should be the time when most of those people you target are active. It can be during the day or night. The best times are before 9 am when people report to work, and after 5-6 pm when people leave work.

Target content to mobile users: Post content that will reach mobile users who use smartphones because they tweet almost throughout the day. They tweet as they eat, as they commute, as they travel and as they are on the go. Tweet them as you ride your bike at the gym, as you commute in the bus or train, during TV commercials, and as you wait for your lunch in the restaurant. They will receive your tweets, respond and retweet them to their followers who may decide to follow you.

Follow people who share your interests, and their followers. Look for people who share your interests and who have many followers, follow them, and then follow their followers. If you like cake baking, include that information on your bio then find people with that interest by searching hashtags. Start engagements by tweeting those users with many followers, then follow them and their followers. These people are more likely to follow you also. However, you should be cautious because following too many people may drive away potential followers.

Direct people to your Twitter account. You can use links like "Follow me on Twitter" on your other social media accounts, website, blog, email address and everywhere on the web to direct followers to your Twitter account. This makes it easy for people to find your profile and follow you especially those who have an interest in what you do. You may want to catch attention by using interesting images, videos or graphics since visual messages are more noticeable than text.

Ask people to retweet you. When you tweet people, you should ask them to retweet you by adding "Please retweet" or "Please RT" at the end of your posts although not on all of them, to avoid appearing spammy. This will help you to get exposure and encourage your followers to share your content as they tweet and retweet, helping to spread your message.

Repeat your most popular tweets. Keep posting the tweets which become popular. Check the tweets, comments and replies on your Twitter name by searching for it and this will help you to see your most popular tweets. Repeat the posts a few times between 8 to 12 hours. You'll catch the attention of those people who may not have seen the updates earlier and this will help you to reach more people every time you do it. Different people browse through their accounts at different times either during the day or nighttime. Some people may not like the repetitions so you may have to stop for some time or go slow on it if you get complaints.

Join a Twitter chat and contribute. When you join any of these groups, you should contribute content that adds value. Every other day, groups talk about certain topics related to their niches or industries. You can get together and talk about various topics when you join any of these chat groups. You will meet new people who will follow you as you share information and learn valuable lessons related to your sector. Some of these will become your followers as you engage with them. Some popular chats are #tchat, #blogchat, #CustServ, #HBRchat, #bufferchat and #mediachat. You can find out about other chats from Chat Salad, Tweets Report and Twubs among other sites.

Get featured on Twitter Counter and Twitaholic: To boost your influence, you need to get featured on these services. You can get real followers on Twitter by getting featured on Twitter Counter and Twitaholic. This is a perfect way to get followers on Twitter and increase your popularity. Twitter marketing campaigns start when you pay for these services and after your purchase has been processed. You will select the number of impressions you wish to purchase and the number will be displayed. These are the number of pageviews you wish Twitter to promote. The amount you are supposed to pay and the number of followers you gain will also be shown. You will be able to manage your marketing campaign and see how you are doing from the report page. You can also target the right audience and schedule campaigns to be able to maximize conversions.

When you join this service, your profile will appear both on Twitter Counter and Twitaholic.com homepages. Any visitor to these sites can follow you. Make sure that what you are sharing is interesting so that people can start talking about it. People can start talking with you and with each other. You will therefore attract high-quality and relevant followers.

Use keywords to find followers: You cannot follow everyone. Conduct keyword research to find what people in your niche or industry are searching and post content based on what is searched. This will help you to attract relevant followers.

Tweet inspirational quotes: People particularly enjoy these quotes and they trigger higher engagement on Twitter as people read them and share them with others. You can use Forismatic which is a free app, to receive many inspiring quotes which you can post to Twitter. This will help you to gain more followers.

Schedule your tweets: You may use Hootsuite and other free and low-cost tools that enable you schedule your tweets beforehand. This ensures consistency of the flow of your tweets and saves time. Followers like to follow people who post content on a regular basis.

Follow users who follow your followers: You can utilize Tweepi and other free and low-cost tools to get a list of accounts that follow your Twitter followers. Follow them because you may share similar interests and they are likely to follow you as well.

Tactics to Gain Fans and Followers on Facebook

Create a Facebook business Page

You may already have a personal account on Facebook, what you therefore need is a business page. If you want to have fans and followers to help you make money on Facebook, on your website or blog, you need to create a Facebook business page.

Why is it important to have many Facebook fans and followers?

- Popularity – a Page with 100,000 followers is more popular than the one with 1,000.

- Trust – Other people will trust your brand if you have many followers.

- More visits – You will attract more traffic and higher search engine rankings.

You need to have friends on your personal Facebook account

You need to share the updates you post on your business page with your friends on your personal account. This increases your exposure, likes and shares which will attract other Facebook users to your Page. There are high chances that your friends on your personal account will "like", comment and "share" your posts and become your friends on your business Page. This will increase your site visitors and also the number of people who see your posts who will start following you.

Sharing these posts on your personal page therefore promotes your business Page which increases the number of friends and fans giving your posts more visibility. You should also invite all your friends and the new friends you are gaining to like your Facebook Page.

Advertise on your Facebook Page

Facebook Pages are public. This means that, whatever you post on your Page can be viewed by anyone. This is one of the best places to get more followers. When you add friends on Facebook, following them and them following you, becomes automatic. Your friends can automatically follow you and you can follow them. Your posts will be sent to their News Feed and their posts will be sent to your News Feed. If you are in business, you may want other people to follow you not just your friends. You want to connect with anyone by having the public see what you offer because you never know who would be interested. You can make your posts and photos public so anyone can view them. This will help you to gain fans and followers who can share your posts with other people widening your online marketplace.

Share posts publicly

Celebrities, public figures and many other influential people are referred to as influencers. You can follow them and they can follow you. When you share your posts publicly, anything you post is sent to your friends' and followers' News Feeds. This has a ripple effect because when they share this with their friends and followers, they help you gain more and more fans and followers. This is a great opportunity to earn money if they like what you are selling to them.

Optimize your Facebook business page

To optimize your Facebook business page:

- choose a catchy page title

- write a suitable description

- post interesting content

This will make it easier for you to attract new followers and more likes which will attract more followers.

Add Facebook "Like" buttons on your website

To gain more fans you should add the "Like" button and "Like box" on your website which are some of the best options you have. For the like button, you should enter your Facebook page URL then edit the button so you can display people's faces, their words, and more information.

Increase engagement

Start sharing interesting and informational content to keep your fans engaged. If they are happy with what you are offering, they may convert to site visitors and then to customers. There are simple rules to follow that will increase engagement on your business page. Share relevant content that your fans look for on your page. Share content that is related to your website, blog or what you are promoting. Don't forget that your followers follow your business page to get your updates. If you want to become social, use your personal Facebook account, not your business page.

Share relevant information not just links

People look everywhere to get information to solve their problems and enhance their lives. Share this information and not just links. If you do this, your Facebook posts will likely get more likes and shares than posts with just links. Give people value, quality and relevant information which is easy to read, in their timelines. This can be a list, and they will likely click the "Like" button because they get useful information without browsing the website.

Share images and videos

Popular Facebook pages share photos, videos and infographics in addition to text postings. This content attracts more "likes", "shares" and comments and as a result, the page gets more fans and followers.

Provide incentives

Why should someone follow you on Facebook instead of other business pages? You need to give followers incentives so they can continue following your business page. These may include frequent updates and contests.

Promote your own content and page

When you create your business page, you should not expect it to get followers instantly. Promote your business page in other places like emails, blogs, on your other social media accounts and on events. Promote your business on other social media networks such as Twitter, Instagram, Google+, Pinterest, LinkedIn and Tumbrl and ask your followers to follow you on Facebook.

Effective Ways to attract Followers on Instagram

- **Fill out your bio:** Your Instagram bio is very important because it tells people who you are so you should include all the details. Let them know why you want them to follow you. Include relevant hashtags related to your brand, niche or industry. Use some hashtags that are related to your content so it can be found when searched. Put your desired call to action so people know right away what is expected of them. Include relevant keywords and links to your other social profiles, blogs and website so Instagram users can also follow you there.

- **Follow others:** If you want people to follow you, you have to follow them. When you like, share and comment on other people's photos, they are likely to do the same in your account. This helps you to gain new followers organically.

- **Go for quality not quantity**: Edit your images so that you post the best on your account. Avoid pointless images which you pick at random.

- **Use popular hashtags**. Use the best hashtags on your photos and videos so people can find you when they search, such as #instagood, #photooftheday and #tbt. Follow people who use popular hashtags such as #likeforlike and #followme or those relevant to your niche because a good number of them will follow you back. Don't use too many hashtags on one photo. Use about 5-7 but not more than 10 hashtags.

- **Target influencers**: Ask influencers to mention your product or website or to tag your product. If you know of any influential user on Instagram who may have used your product, request for a mention because this could win you a ton of new followers.

- **Time**: The most effective time that research studies have shown to be the best time to post photos is at 2 am or 5 pm. Try to post your photos at this time.

- **Ask questions:** Include questions in the captions of your photos to trigger interest and increase engagement. People will start commenting and this may go viral and win you many followers.

- **Connect Instagram with your Facebook account:** Instagram is now owned by Facebook, and if you connect both accounts, it will give you more exposure and win you a lot of potential followers. All your Instagram posts will be seen on Facebook as well. You can connect your accounts using Instagram Settings menu.

- **Research popular hashtags for your niche, brand and industry**: Hashtags are words and short phrases that describe and categorize the image. Hashtags help people search for your image, and can add your image to current trends. Using hashtags is incredibly important to reaching a larger audience

- **Add a few hashtags to each image:** Add a few of the most pertinent hashtags you can find to your image. Try to limit the number of hashtags to 3-10 at the most. If you have too many hashtags, your followers will feel like your images are too spammy.

How You Can Attract Followers on You Tube

- **Upload videos once a week or more often:** To get more subscribers to your videos try as much as possible to provide a lot of content. The more videos you post the more people will watch them and the more popular your channel will be. This will make viewers want to come back and watch more video especially if they are high quality. This will lead to more subscribers. However quality is more important than quantity. Posting too many videos might overwhelm your channel and make it difficult for videos to access the videos they are searching for.

- **Write catchy titles:** Take your time to write good titles that stand out among the countless video search results that take place for You Tube content. Include brand keywords in the title and make it descriptive enough to make it possible for search engines to index it. This means that it will be possible to match the content being searched with the video.

- **Have meaningful descriptions:** Make your videos visible by writing meaningful description that includes relevant keywords. Explain what the video is about and what the viewer should expect from it but avoid overloading it with words that make it difficult to read.

- **Be consistent and stick to your schedule:** Upload and post your videos regularly. Choose particular times in the week to do this. Subscribers need to know when to expect the videos and you stick to your schedule, they are likely to come back to watch them and become subscribers. People like regular videos rather than those posted at random.

- **Tag your videos properly:** Match your video tags with the content so that when a viewer searches for something the video will pop-up. Ensure that the tags you use make it easier for your videos to be visible in relevant searches. Use keywords and phrases.

- **Post attention-grabbing videos:** Deliver quality and value so the viewer will be compelled to watch and keep returning to watch more.

- **Write scripts:** This helps you to deliver consistent content and win more subscribers because the scripts help you to stay in line with the theme of your video.

- **Post content consistently:** You should pair up the content you upload with the theme of your channel so viewers can know what to expect. When you choose to upload recipe videos then stick to that because subscribers will be searching for your videos to watch that particular content. If they don't find it you will likely lose them when the content doesn't match what they expect. If you want to post various topics and themes you should have different channels for each one of them. You should then link your channels to avoid confusing viewers.

- **Interact and engage with your subscribers:** Interacting and engaging with the YouTube community will help you grow. Google and other search engines like these interactions and this will help you appear on top of search results if you it well. Reply to comments positively and delete any negative messages from internet trolls that might irritate subscribers. Make your channel user-friendly and this will make it popular.

- **Subscribe to multiple channels:** Do not restrict yourself to one channel. Find other channels and subscribe to them but make sure that they share your interests. Leave comments that will entice that channel's subscribers to join your channel. Don't spam those other channels with your videos otherwise you might be blocked or viewers will ignore your videos.

- **Advertise your channel:** Use your other social media accounts, websites, blogs and emails to advertise your channel. Let all your friends and followers in different social networks that you use know about your new videos.

Chapter 8:
How to get the most from social media marketing

To build wealth, you need to keep up with social media and use it effectively. Most businesses today, create at least one social media profile to become visible. Others create multiple accounts to spring up their marketing campaigns. That is why there has been a significant increase of businesses that use social media, especially in the recent past. If you still struggle to understand how you can take advantage of social media, you are not alone.

What is social media marketing?

Social media marketing is the process of building awareness about you, your products or services through the various social media channels. The ultimate goal of any social media marketing campaign is to drive traffic to a website, increase the visibility of a product, gain more social media followers or find more customers.

Why is social media marketing important?

Social Media marketing is important because:

- Business has become social - with many people using social media accounts as their main websites.

- Social media is the new marketing - Today, people spend a lot of time on social media and you have to get them there when marketing yourself, your brand, products or services.

- It is fast - this is the fastest way that you can use to spread word around using fans and followers. A tweet, Facebook post, Instagram photo, You Tube video can become viral in a few minutes. Spreading a message this way is even faster than use TV and print media advertisements.

- It has become the new influencer - with many companies reporting that they have gained new customers from Twitter, Facebook or other social networks.

- It is the new trend – people who spend their time on social media reaches millions of active users daily. This is where you'll find them when you need them.

Social media marketing has for sure dominated the major social platforms to say the least. These social networks boast of millions of active users from all over the world with most of them actively logging into their accounts daily. This can proved by the millions of tweets posted every day on Twitter, the mammoth of daily posts on Facebook and billions of YouTube daily views. This is strengthened by the excitement that Instagram photo sharing has caused which goes on every other minute.

Strategies You Can Use in Social Media Marketing

Social media networks have enabled all kinds of businesses to interact directly with consumers. This makes it easier to promote and sell products and services directly. Whether you are an individual or a business, you can now boost your sales and revenue through social media platform and drive traffic to your site and business pages. There is nothing to prevent you from utilizing social media sites to your advantage whether it is Twitter, Facebook, Google+, LinkedIn, You Tube, Instagram, Tumblr, Pinterest or MySpace.com among many others.

To boost sales and revenue, you can leverage social media platforms and utilize the great opportunity they offer. You can start and expand your business by building authentic relationships with customers and prospects, as well as encouraging engagements which can lead to offline and online sales.

Sell benefits that your products or services provide

The most important point to ponder when launching your marketing campaign is to focus on how you will help your target audience. This should guide you while laying out your marketing strategy. How will the target audience benefit from your products or services? How will they feel when they use them? What difference will it make? You need to convey an interesting message which will excite your target audience and follow it up with quality products or services which will give them an experience like none other. When you concentrate so much on the features of your products or services, people don't take much interest. But, when you tell them the benefits they will get and how they will feel after using them, they will become curious and want to know more.

Choose the social media platforms you want to use

You need to choose the social media platform where your target audience is and concentrate all your efforts there rather than working on all platforms at the same time. This is important especially if you are a beginner. Once you master one platform then move to the other one and work progressively. Find out the platform most suited to your niche. This is where most of the influencers or leaders in that sector or industry become successful. You can check the number of Twitter or Instagram followers, Facebook fans, You Tube subscribers, Google+ or Pinterest followers they have. If they have 1 million

Facebook fans as compared with 100,000 Twitter followers then it shows that FB is more suitable for your niche than Twitter so you should concentrate your time and efforts. You can use your time efficiently and engage your audience on FB instead of other platforms.

Optimize your social media profiles

You should optimize your profiles on the social platforms you wish to use. This boosts your search engine optimization (SEO) increasing your chances of higher search engine rankings.

This will make you visible to help you gain more followers.

- Use a photo showing your face or an image of your brand. Avoid using things that are not real because you may be regarded as spammy. Social media is about connecting with other people who want to know who you are, by seeing your face clearly.

- Write a good bio with full description about yourself or your company. This may include your background, expertise etc.

- You may indicate what kind of information you intend to share to keep users checking your profile keen.

Go where you will find your customers

To succeed in your social media marketing strategies, you have to go where your prospects are to be able to interact with them. If they are on Facebook, go there, if they are on Twitter find them there etc. Choose the right social networking sites where you will find them regardless of which industry you are in or how big or small your business is.

You can research and find the online community where you target audience can be found if you:

- Monitor social media sites: You can find out which social media sites your customers and prospects use and then market your brand there. To boost your business, find out where your brand and similar brands are being discussed and target that market.

- Enquire from customers: Ask customers which social networks they use and follow them there. Send a survey and check the responses. When you find them make sure that you connect with them and don't allow them to slip away. Find out what their needs are and provide products and services to meet those needs. Give them links to your website and make a follow-up with email or more social posts.

Have interesting conversations and engage your target audience

You should post content depending on the demographics you are targeting. Post interesting content, colorful pictures and funny jokes if you aim to reach the young people, tweets that cover interesting topics and entertaining videos which your fans and followers will engage with. The content can be interesting, emotional, emphatic or even controversial (if that is your stuff) to trigger interest and conversations. You can even ask a question to trigger interest. The content should be relevant to your audience and represent what you are offering in a unique way. Example: Funny videos about tongue cleaners were used by Orabrush to connect with their followers.

Trigger social shares and likes as you increase your social reach

The other thing you should do is to increase your social reach. Social reach is the engagement you have with your fans and followers. If you have something that triggers social engagement you will have more social shares and likes. This will help you to rank highly on search engine results and make you visible. You will have a strong online presence. This will increase sales and revenue since the online traffic can find you easily. Business is about traffic. Without traffic and SEO to make you noticed, you may not get to where you want to go.

Share interesting and relevant content

You may have heard that content is king and that is the same in social media. This is the foundation that you lay for successful social media marketing campaigns. If you share useful content that is also interesting you will likely get more retweets, likes, comments, re-shares and more visitors to your website or blog who can convert to customers.

Content may include:

- Catchy profiles, photos and videos.

- Catchy headlines, titles and descriptions.

- Articles and stories related to your niche on various topics.

- Questions to trigger interest.

- Motivational Quotes and answers to questions which are either related to your niche or other information.

- Funny jokes, images and videos as well as other interesting stuff which your followers will enjoy.

- Hashtags to make your content searchable.

- Interesting statistics and research studies about your niche.

Use Thumbnails to increase YouTube views

When you get more views on your You Tube videos, your business grows. However, because of the immense videos on You Tube, some of them may end up not being watched and this is why you should seek more legitimate views. Using thumbnails that grab attention is one of the easiest ways to increase views. Make the video thumbnails compelling and a "must-watch".

Create powerful thumbnails by using:

- Text: Use compelling words within the thumbnail so your viewers can know right away what the video is about by glancing at it. You should also tell viewers why they should watch it within the description.

- Catchy title and description: Make the text or description easy to read. Usually, the text is on the right side of the thumbnail while the image is on the left.

- Graphics: Use your face or head shot so you can give your thumbnail a personal touch. Add a colorful background so you can grab the attention of viewers.

- Emotion: Find a way to put emotion within your thumbnails. By showing expression on the face you have used it makes it intriguing i.e. let it to look like that person is happy, disgusted, shocked, amazed or whatever you want to represent. If the expression intrigues the audience, sure enough people will click the image to know more.

Start with a few Social Media Platforms

Start posting on 3-4 social media platforms and build your presence there then move to the others. Having a strong presence in a few networks is better than posting on the countless platforms. Build a strong presence on these networks promotes you better than having an average presence in many of them. Post your content where your audience hangs out. Join online groups which are based on your niche or industry, to find out if your target audience hangs out on that platform. Concentrate on posting content on platforms where that audience spends most of the time. This will benefit your business especially if the active members engage on topics which you focus on.

Link your social media pages with your website or blog

After getting your social media profiles ready, you should link them with one another and with your website or blog if you have one. You can promote your brand on your social media business pages the same way you use a website.

Interlink all your social media accounts

There are many sites you can set your business profiles on, such as Facebook, Twitter, Instagram, Google+, Pinterest, You Tube, LinkedIn and Snapchat among others. Mention your social media profiles on all the sites you have accounts and share the content across all the social networks.

Stay above the competition

You should never ignore your competition. If you do, it will be to your detriment. Conduct a survey of your competitors on social media networks by checking the social sites in which they are most active and move there. Check what content they publish on social media sites and post similar or better content but don't post duplicate content.

Find out how they market their products or services on social media and imitate them. Find how many customers, fans, "likes", "shares" and views they receive on each social site and lay a strategy to exceed them. Do better than them and you will stay ahead.

Refresh the content to make it interesting as you promote products

Market your products by creating authentic relationships with people but don't push them to buy them. Target people who are related to your niche or industry, who influence the online community. Seek out celebrities, famous people, popular bloggers, successful webmasters and popular fans with things which will catch their attention. If they like, share or mention you or your products, this will drive a flow of traffic to your site or pages.

Promote offers on social media sites

To gain followers on social media channels, you need to post exclusive offers which they won't be able to get elsewhere. Post contests for those who LIKE, coupons, discounts and special offers. Post external news, free shipping and new product announcements through their News Feed.

Google Analytics

Google Analytics is an important tool that enables you to keep track of what people are searching for on your website. If you know what people are looking for, then you are able to serve them better. Utilize Google Analytics to find out what people are saying about your site and use the keywords they are searching for to fulfill their needs and wants. This is the only way you can monitor your progress, improve your site and make it successful.

Grow by offering free content

As much as 90% of purchasing decisions start when people search for products and services online according to Forrester research. You should therefore post relevant, useful and quality content from which prospects can know more about your products or services. You may think that you are giving away your best content for free in exchange for nothing but this is not true, in fact you gain a lot. The more people know about you and what you offer the more likely that they will buy from you. Prospects become willing to buy your products or services when they see the high quality free content. They feel more confident and trust you, because they associate the quality of the content with the value they are paying for.

You will therefore grow your business when you offer your best content for free because prospects will associate you with great value. This will build trust and they will become confident because of the high value you deliver in your content. When you are creating content, think about your target audience's problems and try to solve them with your products or services, social media posts, videos, articles, blog posts, infographics, webinars, and podcasts. Posting great content for free gives you a chance to educate your potential prospects about your brand. This portrays you as the solution to their problems. Content marketing begin your authentic relationships with your prospective customers.

Identify and engage influencers

You can use influencers to raise awareness about your brand, products or services. Influencers include internal and external ones. You can ask your employees to post on social media about your brands because they understand it better and they can promote your business and answer any questions customers may have. Influencers whether they are internal or external ensure can greatly influence the online community in your favor. Ensure that you leverage their influence so that they can spread word-of-mouth to influence sales and revenue. This can make your profits soar suddenly. One of the ways to do this, is to segment your customers so that internal influencers can engage with them by targeting specific marketing campaigns to a particular category and rewarding them for taking the desired action.

There are various tools that you can use to connect with external influencers. These tools include Traackr, Klout, PeekYou, mBlast, Kred by peoplebrowsr, and PeerIndex among others. Avoid picking popular influencers who have a high number of followers but don't have an influence on your target audience.

Research Popular Content posted by Your Competitors

Check content posted by competitors which is popualor among the audience of your and create similar posts which will be popular to your audience. Don't copy content, but create around the same topic in a different way.

Utilize Twitter Advanced Search

The Twitter Advanced Search helps you to find prospects who want to buy your products or services and those who want o know if they can solve their problems. You only type in the word or phrase

Connect with Mobile Users

To improve the impact of your social media efforts target mobile users with mobile-friendly content. Target promoted posts specifically for smartphones. When you target people on mobile devices, you get them when they are here and about.

Chapter 9:
Parting Shots

Today, social media is playing an important role in e-commerce than ever before. Social media networks have been widely recognized all over the world as marketing opportunities. When fans and followers interact they share about your brand and products or products, which strengthens SEO and your site becomes visible. All you need to do is to make sure that, your business pages contain interesting content which can be shared easily.

How to update content regularly, measure results and keep improving

Throughout this book, you have seen how you can make social media work for you. However, you cannot be successful everywhere. You need to determine the right platforms for you and your target audience. The success of your social media goals and strategies depend on the platforms where your fans and followers are based, whether it is on Twitter, Facebook, You Tube or Instagram as well as Pinterest, Google +, Tunblr and LinkedIn. Find out where your audience spends their time so you can position your marketing campaign to be successful on different platforms.

Create useful and interesting content

Any content that customers will find useful will attract them. Show them how your products or services can help them solve problems in their lives. Make the content interesting and interactive enough to keep them engaged. This will attract new site visitors and keep existing customers wanting to know more if they find it interesting. The content should be informative, useful and unique. Find out what demographics you want to serve so you can offer appropriate content which they will find interesting. For example, men enjoy watching videos while teenagers are most times on their mobile devices. Post entertaining content on social media and encourage sharing and conversations.

Contribute towards discussions that take place on online forums which are related to your niche market or business. Send useful and interesting answers to questions and quote your URL so users will seek your content. This may lead them to your site as they use the links you have provided.

Update your content regularly

Fans buy what they can share with their friends and followers to find out what they think. You should therefore post user-friendly content which will make your friends and followers "like" and share your content. They will comment on photos, videos, tweets and send product reviews among other things. This is good for you because Google loves user-generated content.

You should encourage users to "like", "share" content and make comments on a continuous basis because search engines keep coming back to spider the pages. Fresh content and high-quality links raise your position on Google and other search engine ranking results. Search engine spiders detect fresh content immediately it is posted. Post fresh content which triggers interest to encourage fans and followers to keep posting user-generated content.

If you have a physical store, shoppers will see the products and enquire about them. This is the same online. Your products may be your posts, physical products or services, digital goods, knowledge or information. If posts are your products, then people will ask what they want to know before they make decisions. Post high-quality photos, videos, audio, product descriptions and other content.

If you have a website or online store, you can take photo or videos that clearly show the products. You can post the benefits derived from using these products or include the information on product descriptions. State the value they add to people's lives and how they will solve their problems.

Measure results and keep improving

Use Google Analytics to measure results against the goals you set. This will help you to find out if you are achieving them or not. Make adjustments where necessary to improve performance. Set goals based on each type of content and then check tweets, retweets, shares, likes, comments and product reviews and ratings to know what fans are saying. Find out what type of content is effective and use it more often and discard what is not leading to conversions but before you do so, find out why and refine the content. Find out what appeals to your audience and what is shared on social media and concentrate you efforts here.

If you do not measure results you will not know what works and what doesn't. Be creative and use humor when you write content. It may not necessarily be about your products it may be about your everyday life or something you are passionate about, especially if you are dealing with a niche you enjoy. Post blogs and articles about your niche products which customers may not find elsewhere but make your content interesting and entertaining.

Smart tracking and measuring is needed to fully capture the benefit of a social media campaign and while looking for direct ROI is one way to do it, there are other values to be measure from social media marketing.

When you participate in social media you not only benefit from the income you earn but you improve customer service and boost public relations. To know whether your social media marketing campaigns have been successful you need to track and measure social reach, flow of traffic, lead generation, the number of fans and followers, subscriptions and conversion rates. Whatever these metrics show just know there is always room for improvement so, you should not stagnate. However, the income you earn is passive which means that after you have done what this book recommends, you will earn profits with little effort.

Optimize Websites, Blogs and Other Outlets

If you have a website or blog you need to popularize it through social media. This is to attract traffic. In the online marketplace you need a regular flow of traffic to your website or blog if you are to make profits and succeed. The site visitors who convert to become buyers will make your online business to thrive.

An online store or blog is not like a brick-and-mortar store which passers-by can see and stop over to buy what you are selling. In an online business prospects, may not even notice you are there and that is why social media networks are handy. They popularize your online store or blog by doing what most people enjoy such as tweeting, retweeting, writing what you like, posting photos, shooting videos and having conversations and sharing in the discussions all for free.

You need to be visible for traffic to flow to the site and then find ways to convert the site visitors to buyers. Many people concentrate their efforts on SEO so that Google, Bing and Yahoo! can rank them on top of ranking results. This drives traffic to their sites once they are noticeable.

You can also post blogs to promote your brand. Choose topics that talk about your brand, niche or industry. If you create interesting blogs, people will look out for them regularly. Make sure that they cover areas that people have an interest in. If you cannot write a blog then tweet. Tweets are mini-blogs which are very popular.

How to attract traffic to your site

Content is king and this also applies to social media marketing. It has to be unique, high-quality and useful to users so that your site can be placed on top of ranking results. Low-quality content and duplicate content is disregarded. The PageRank of your site depends on several factors.

These include:

- The page layout

- Genuine customer experiences

- Product reviews and ratings

- The time durations site visitors spend on your site

- Your conversion rates

- Whether you have diverse traffic

- Unique product descriptions

Encourage your site visitors to leave likes, shares, comments and product reviews, on the site and on social media to generate more traffic. If you get more traffic, you get more conversions, higher sales and revenue which means higher profits.

Make product pages detailed

Product pages attract search engine spiders, which look for PageViews and this translates to more site visitors or higher traffic. You therefore need to put as many details as possible on the product pages of your e-Commerce site. The content you post on the product pages is crucial because customers visit the product page to view these details. These include product images, product descriptions, comments, reviews and ratings, price, benefits derived from using the products or services, coupons, discounts, and other offers. They use this information to decide whether to buy or not to buy the product. If they decide to buy, they click the "add to cart" button.

Search engines use the content on the product pages to rank sites in their ranking results. The product pages are therefore so important because they lead to conversions on high-ranking sites. You should optimize your website by including all the relevant details such as catchy titles, compelling text, brand names, images, tags, prices, product sizes, colors and more information to help shoppers make decisions. This is based on search engine rankings and so, you should ensure that the product pages can be indexed to make them visible and easily available on-site queries.

You have to optimize your site by customizing it and improving the details on the product pages to attract your target audience. Submit URLs containing which contain relevant keywords to popular search engines, encourage user-generated content, mark as Noindex on product pages which you wouldn't want to be indexed and use Nofollow on all the links that you don't want to be followed.

Choose an efficient e-commerce solution

The e-commerce solution you choose work effectively and efficiently. The shopping cart should be user-friendly to hasten the checkout process otherwise if it is slow, you will have more shopping cart abandonment rates. The load times should be fast because if it is slow, many people become impatient. As a result, they leave the shopping carts without making purchases and move to sites that load faster.

The e-commerce solution should also process payments fast, update products regularly and make navigation by site visitors who visit the website pages, easy.

Encourage shoppers to complete the checkout process

To increase your online sales you need to encourage shoppers to complete the checkout process. Entice your customers with offers which they get at the end of the checkout process. This will boost your business, but you also need to simplify the checkout process and make it fast, so shoppers can complete their purchases. Ask the most relevant questions that you need such as credit card details, phone number, and shipping information.

Adopt SEO techniques that work

Successful businesses adopt SEO techniques and concepts that spell success for them. SEO as we have seen earlier in this book improves site rankings, increases traffic to your site and this ultimately increases sales and revenue and profits rise.

In order to realize higher ROI for your business, you need to bring prospects as near as possible to close a sale by doing the following:

Optimize product pages with SEO

Displaying your brands on your website isn't enough. You also need to optimize the products for search engine rankings, in order to make them visible.

- Include the product name within the title

- Include the product name in the description or text

- Include the product name in the URL

- Use different colors on each product page

- Base product categories on how they are searches

- Use relevant keywords in the links

Prioritize your products

Put your main products on the homepage to catch attention of traffic and display them on your social media accounts with your website's URL. The main products are the ones that generate sales. If you can't display them on the homepage of your site where they can be indexed then display links that lead to the product pages both on the home page and on social media platforms. This will encourage indexing but target your marketing campaigns on products that sell most which generate the highest revenue.

Utilize Google Analytics

When you use Google Analytics, it helps you to know what works and what doesn't. It enables you to measure success for each social media platform and marketing campaign, as well for each type of content that you post, so you can know where to invest more of your money, time and efforts. efforts.

Prioritize your products

Focus your attention on the main products that generate sales and place them on the homepage of your site or put links that lead to the product pages if they aren't on the homepage. This will make them visible and be available for indexing. Target your marketing strategies on the products that sell most and generate revenue.

Offer free but useful resources

People like free things especially if they are useful resources. This can be a free iPod, iPhone, samples, mobile application or discounts. This will make site visitors to visit your site to get the free resources and this encourages them to make purchases. You will attract prospects as you retain your existing customers. To make people to want these resources, they should be things they are willing to pay for, but they are free which creates a lot of excitement which can cause a buzz. People will share the information on social media and as a result your sales and profits will rise and you will gain fans and followers as well.

Post social contests

You can post contests on different social media platforms and display your links to your website and blog there. These contests cause a lot of excitement and people start conversations about them. They have the tendency to can create a buzz on social media sites and which can drive a large flow of traffic to your site.

How to Increase Revenue and Maximize Profits Using Social Media

There are many strategies that Increase online sales and revenue

You may have drawn traffic to your site, but you need to maximize sales. You can do this using the following strategies:-

- Optimize content

- Increase conversion rates

- Encourage customers to checkout

Optimize content

The content you post should be original and high-quality otherwise you may be penalized by Google and other search engines. Repeating keywords or copying content may be penalized as spam. You should keep watching changes in Google algorithms so you can stay ahead of your competitors on search engine ranking results. Ensure that you post unique and useful content. Keep refreshing it for search engine indexing and this will lead to higher profits when your target audience notices you. Create a checklist and schedule your content on each social network to know where you will share which content.

Utilize team effort

We all need each other. Create a team including your partners, managers, employees and business employees to work together. Each team members has a network fans and followers they can share your content with. Utilize this opportunity although it require coordination to be effective. Set social media guidelines so that everyone knows what, when and how to share the content. Train your team members and use various messages to suit everyone's kind of audience. You can even write scripts to be followed for consistency purposes.

Interview influencers who are experts

In all industries, there are some people who influence trends and major decisions that impact success. You need to get these people and involve them if you want to dominate social media platforms. These people will set your brand, products, services or company apart from the rest and help you to stand out. If you get the chance, you can interview influencers who are experts in your field or industry. Try to make them interested in sharing your content by interviewing them on your blog or elsewhere. People will take interest in the content which will lead to more sales and revenue.

Involve influencers

To leverage influencers in your niche or industry you can reciprocate the favor of sharing your content. This will help you to cultivate strong relationships with the influencers although this might take time. Keep in touch with them through other channels like emails because they will influence your business success.

Use social media to broadcast

Social media is your broadcast channel and it is so effective that, if you do it as recommended in this book it will serve as a bait to attract success. It will pull traffic to your content, and if it is interesting, original and useful, it will gain you reputation on social media and you will command authority and become a leader. It will maximize your profits in a way that you never thought it could.

Be precise

Your content should be precise since you are dealing with people who are busy with their lives. You don't want your target audience to spend time on your social profiles or websites trying to get what you want to say. They may not have all the time because they also have their own lives to live away from your social account, blog or website. Don't make the content overwhelming, keep it concise. Write short sentences that state a point or idea in each paragraph. Don't keep elaborating otherwise people may lose interest in reading the content.

Inspire your target audience to take action

You may put in a lot of your money, time and efforts, but if you don't let people know what you want them to do, your marketing campaigns may not succeed. Tell them clearly to like your photos on Instagram, subscribe to your You Tube videos, share your tweets on Twitter, comment on your Facebook posts or follow you. Display your desired call to action in a strategic place where everyone can see it.

This book cannot end without mentioning the mistakes you should avoid.

Social media mistakes you should avoid

The following are the mistakes people do so if you can avoid them you will save your money, time and effort. You will also become successful much faster.

Don't concentrate on Facebook only

There are people who post on Facebook only while there are other social networks which you can use to promote your products, services, website or blog. You may create a personal profile on Facebook but you need other social media platforms for SEO.

Posting on many social media platforms

Concentrating on Facebook is one extreme while posting on too many social networks is the other extreme. To achieve good results, you need to create strong presence in 3-4 platforms and once you are sure of your engagements move on to other platforms. You should know that after some point your profiles on those social media platforms where you have a strong presence will grow organically and your effort will pay-off enabling you to shift to other networks.

Failing to optimize social media profiles for SEO

SEO helps your business to gain visibility and attract traffic but these are not the only benefits. SEO boosts your online presence on both search engine rankings and social media. It also improves your brand's public relations (PR) and customer service.

Having no social media buttons on the website or blog

Social media buttons spell success for your business because site visitors are able to share your content easily on social media. The social buttons should therefore be displayed in strategic positions on your website or blog where everyone can easily see them. These buttons should be in a size that stands out.

Sharing content from your website only

You need to share content from other websites not just your website. The main purpose of social media platforms is to network with users and share interesting content from many websites. This is one of the best ways you can get noticed and increase your followers. Follow the influencers and leaders in your niche or industry and share their content with others on your social media accounts. Do this consistently. Find ways to interact with them by posting likes, shares and comments or mention them in your posts.

You get followed but you don't follow back

You need to follow those who follow you. If you don't reciprocate, by following those that are already following you This is another common mistake most beginners do with social media. They put all their efforts in following new people or removing those who are not following them back and forget to follow back those that are already following them.

Personal profile vs. business profile

There are people who create a personal profile and think it is a business profile. Except Twitter where you can promote your business in the same account, you need to have a Business page on Facebook, Google+ for business in Google and Pinterest for Business on Pinterest. You need to create a personal profile first on Facebook and Google+.

Forget to engage with fans and followers

Social networks are for connecting and engaging with other people. Don't forget to engage because that is how you find new customers and more fans and followers. You may follow them but you also need to engage with them personally. This is very effective and it boosts your business whether it is online or offline.

Assuming all who like your posts visit your website

There are people who "like" your posts but may not visit your website.

Using no images with the posts

People are inclined to visual images rather than text messages. Posts that use nice photos and videos attract more likes, shares, tweets, and Pins because they trigger interest. Compliment your posts with high quality images because as they say, a picture represents a thousand words and this is even better when you use high-quality videos.

Failure to use hashtags

Using hashtags is one of the easiest ways to follow conversations. If you don't use hashtags, it becomes very difficult from your fans and followers to follow these discussions on the platforms you post on. Use relevant hashtags which are related to your brand, niche, field and industry. Use a keyword that is straightforward.

There are rules that every social media platform follows. When you send your posts, they may not be seen by all you fans and followers. That is why

SEO and marketing campaigns are important to help you to become more visible.

Conclusion

Marketing strategies have changed with the advancement in technology. People are now communicating more using social media than ever before. Customers and prospects can communicate with you anywhere at any time on social media networks. Social media offers you the greatest platforms to sell your products, services, knowledge and whatever else you have.

There are still business owners and marketers out there, who still don't know how to leverage on social media. They may use their personal accounts to interact with others but they don't know how to make passive income using the most popular social media networks Twitter, Facebook, Instagram and YouTube. I am sure you have learnt a lot in this book and all you need now is to implement what has been recommended. If you follow these guidelines you will earn a stream flow of income, passively.

www.ingramcontent.com/pod-product-compliance
Lightning Source LLC
Chambersburg PA
CBHW071117050326
40690CB00008B/1244